BEGINNING
CHESS
PLAY

ABOUT THE AUTHOR

Bill Robertie is a chess master and a former winner of the US Chess Speed Championships;. He is also the world's best backgammon player and the only two-time winner of the Monte Carlo World Championships. Besides authoring two books on chess, the first in a series of more than 10 titles in *The Road to Chess Mastery Series*, he's written five books on backgammon and is the co-publisher of *Inside Backgammon*, the world's foremost backgammon magazine.

His club and tournament winnings from chess and backgammon allow Robertie to travel the world in style. Robertie currently makes his home in Arlington, Massachusetts.

Chess and Backgammon Books by Bill Robertie

Beginning Chess Play
Winning Chess Openings
Backgammon for Winners
Advanced Backgammon Volume 1: Positional Play
Advanced Backgammon Volume 2: Technical Play
Lee Genud vs. Joe Dwek
Reno 1986

BEGINNING CHESS PLAY

BILL ROBERTIE

- ROAD TO CHESS MASTERY -
CARDOZA PUBLISHING

First Edition

Library of Congress Catalog Card No: 94-70604
ISBN: 0-940685-50-7

CARDOZA PUBLISHING
P.O. Box 1500, Cooper Station, New York, NY 10276 • (718)743-5229

Write for your <u>free</u> catalogue of gaming books, advanced strategies and computer games.

TABLE OF CONTENTS

1. INTRODUCTION   7

2. THE BASICS OF CHESS   9
The Board and the Pieces
Identifying the Chess Pieces
Setting Up the Board
How the Game is Played

3. HOW THE PIECES MOVE   13
The King
The Rook
The Bishop
The Queen
The Knight
The Pawn
Pawn Promotion
En Passant
Castling
Relative Value of the Pieces

4. CHECK & CHECKMATE   33
Checkmate
Checkmate Strategy

5. CHESS NOTATION   43
Abbreviations for the Pieces
Special Notations

6. DRAWN GAMES   49
Stalemate
Perpetual Check
Other Drawn Games

7. GENERAL WINNING STRATEGY   53
Opening, Middle and Endgame Overview
Opening Game Strategy
Order of Opening Development
The Middle Game - Tactics
The Pin
The Fork
Discovered Attacks
The Endgame

8. SAMPLE GAME - DEVELOPMENT STRATEGY 67

Preview
The Game
White Errors & Black Response
Developing the Center
Black Continues Developing
Black Begins the Attack
The First Capture is Made
Discovered Attack!
Evaluating the Position
Playing On
The Queen and the Canter
White Gets Aggressive
Strategy with a Winning Advantage
Black Marches On
The Final Attacks
Analyzing the Game

9. SAMPLE GAME - STRATEGY, TACTICS & MATE! 95

Preview
Opening with the Queen's Pawn
The Queen's Gambit
Early StrategicThinking
The Opening Develops
Check? or Not to Check?
The Pawn Trap
The Isolated Pawn
The Pin!
Mid-Game Analysis
Counter-Attack
Active vs. Passive Chess
Combinations
The Pawn is Captured
The Exchange
Endgame Objectives
The End Game in Motion
Good Moves and Bad Moves
Blunder!!
White's End Game Strategy
The Marching Pawns
White Gets a Decisive Edge
The Coup de Grace!

10. JOINING A CHESS CLUB 135

11. TOURNAMENTS, RATINGS, & THE CHESS CLOCK 137

1. INTRODUCTION

Chess is one of the oldest, most fascinating, and most complex games known to mankind. It's a game of reason and logic, where you win by outthinking, outplanning, and outsmarting your opponent. Unlike some other games, when you beat an opponent he can't say he was unlucky.

In this book, we'll show all you need to know to play and win at chess: from the rules of the game and how to move your pieces, to checkmating your opponent and how a game can end in a draw. Our approach, with plenty of diagrams and clear explanations, makes learning the basics simple and easy. In one quick session, you'll know how to play the game.

We'll take you on a move-by-move journey through two actual games and introduce key concepts like center control, pins, and double attacks. You'll learn these ideas not by studying them in the abstract, but by seeing them in action. You'll also see how you can use an advantage as small as a single pawn to finish off your opponent - a key idea that's at the basis of winning strategy. By the time you finish this book you'll have a firm grounding in the basics of the game, and be able to more than hold your own against most of the players you'll encounter.

We'll also introduce you to the world of chess clubs and tournaments, and you'll see how to find out about clubs in your area, and how to start a club if there isn't one nearby.

Everything you need to get started in chess is in this book. Put it into practice, and you'll start out a winner from the beginning!

2. THE BASICS OF CHESS

THE BOARD AND THE PIECES

Chess is a war game, played between two armies. You're in command of one army, your opponent controls the other.

Your armies meet on a battleground called a **chessboard**. It's an 8 by 8 board with 64 squares, alternating in color between light and dark squares. It's slightly different from a checker board, although you could use a checker board to play if you had to. On a checkerboard, the squares are usually red and black. On a true chessboard, they're white and black, or light wood and dark wood if the board is made of wood.

The armies are called **White** and **Black**. Each army consists of 16 pieces. In Diagram 1, I've listed the different types of pieces, along with the standard symbols that we'll use in this book for the White and the Black pieces.

One King:	♔	♚
One Queen:	♕	♛
Two Rooks:	♖ ♖	♜ ♜
Two Bishops:	♗ ♗	♝ ♝
Two Knights:	♘ ♘	♞ ♞
Eight pawns:	♙ ♙ ♙ ♙ ♙ ♙ ♙	♟ ♟ ♟ ♟ ♟ ♟ ♟

Diagram 1: The chess pieces

Each side has a King and a Queen, two each of Knights, Bishops and Rooks, and eight pawns. You can identify the pieces as follows:

IDENTIFYING THE CHESS PIECES

• The **King** is the tallest piece, usually with a small cross on top.

• The **Queen** is the next tallest piece, with a crown usually having eight points.

• The **Rooks** are generally shaped like towers. On very old sets, the rooks may appear as elephants with towers on their backs.

• The **Bishops** have one distinguishing characteristic: a small notch in the top of the piece, which is supposed to represent a bishop's miter.

• The **Knights** are easy: they resemble a horse's head.

• The **pawns** are the smallest piece, and there are a lot of them: eight for each side.

SETTING UP THE BOARD

The next diagram shows how the pieces are arranged at the start of the game.

Diagram 2: The initial set-up

SETTING UP THE BOARD

Here are a few tips that will help you set up the board correctly each time.

• **White in the right.** Always set up the board with a white square in White's right-hand corner.

• **Queen on color.** The White Queen and King sit on the two middle squares in the first row. The White Queen sits on a white square. (So the King, of course, is on a dark square.)

• **Similar pieces face each other.** The White Queen faces the Black Queen; the White King faces the Black King; and similarly for the other pieces.

• **Rooks in the corner.** The Rooks are the square, tower-like pieces; make sure they sit in the four corners of the board.

• **Bishops next to royalty.** In Medieval times, the Bishops often advised the royal family. Make sure your Bishops sit next to the King and Queen.

HOW THE GAME IS PLAYED

Players generally draw lots to see who plays White and who plays Black. One common way of doing this is to have one player take a White pawn and a Black one and conceal them, one in each hand. The other player then chooses a hand. Alternatively, the players can toss a coin.

Players sit at opposite sides of the board and take turns moving their pieces. By convention, White always moves first. (It wasn't always so. Up until the nineteenth century, players would draw for both color and the right to move first.) Moving first is usually insignificant among beginners, but becomes an important advantage at higher levels.

You may move your pieces either to unoccupied squares or to squares occupied by your opponent's pieces. When you move to a square holding one of your opponent's pieces, you **capture** that piece and remove it from the board and out of play. You cannot however, move your pieces off the board or to a square occupied by one of your own pieces.

Play continues until one player checkmates the other (we'll see how to do that a bit later), someone concedes, or until the game ends in a draw.

Many players play with what is called the **touch-move** rule: if you touch a piece, you must move it if legally possible. This might seem uncomfortable at first, but we recommend that you try to play this way in your own games, as it eliminates arguments. All tournaments are played with the touch-move rule.

That's all there is to it! Now let's push on and see how the individual pieces move.

3. HOW THE PIECES MOVE

THE KING

The King is the most important piece on the board. When the King is threatened with capture, and cannot escape, the game is over. The survival of your whole army depends on your King's safety, so you will need to guard him carefully.

Unfortunately for the King's safety, he is not the most powerful piece on the board - only the most vital. In fact, his powers of movement are quite limited compared to some of the other pieces, as we shall see.

Take a look at Diagram 3.

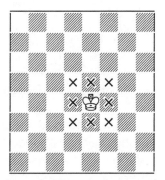

Diagram 3: How the King moves

The White King can move to any one of the eight squares marked with an 'x'. That is, he can move one square in any direction, but only one square. Suppose he chose to move one square to the right. In that case, he would be in the position shown in Diagram 4.

Diagram 4: After a King move

The King movement can be restricted by his own pieces. If a White piece or Pawn occupies a square adjacent to the White King, the King cannot move to that square. Look at Diagram 5.

Diagram 5: Blocked by his own pieces

In Diagram 3, the White King had a total of eight possible moves. But in Diagram 5, the King only has one move! Since he's on a square on the edge of the board, he has at most five possible moves, since there are only five adjacent squares. But four of those squares are occupied by other White pieces. The King can't push his own men aside to make a move. So the only square he can move to is the open black square diagonally up from his position. The presence of his own pieces has drastically reduced his options.

The King captures the same way he moves. He can capture an enemy piece located on any adjacent square. Take a look at Diagram 6.

Diagram 6: How the King captures

The White King has a choice of capturing any of the four Black pieces. He can move one square to his left and capture the Black Bishop, or one square diagonally up to the left and capture a Black Knight, or one square down diagonally to the left to capture the other Black Knight, or one square diagonally to the right to capture the Black pawn. Note that he cannot capture the Black Rook; the Rook is too far away, outside the King's range.

Diagram 7: The King has captured the Black Bishop

THE ROOK

The Rook is a powerful piece, one of the workhorses of your army. The Rook moves in straight lines, forward and backward, left and right. Diagram 8 shows the Rook's movement.

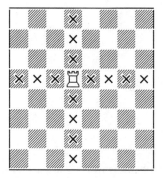

Diagram 8: How the Rook moves

Like the King, the Rook can be blocked from moving by its own pieces. In Diagram 9, the Rook in the corner can move to any of the squares along the first row of the board, but it cannot move up the board because it is blocked by its own pawn.

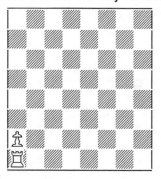

Diagram 9: Rook blocked by a pawn

Below, the White Rook can capture the Black Queen, by moving four squares up the board, or the Black Knight, by moving three squares to the left, or the Black Bishop, by moving three squares down. It cannot, however, capture the Black Rook. Its own Knight blocks it from moving to the right.

Diagram 10: How the Rook captures

THE BISHOP

The Bishop is a nimble piece, with a range almost equal to the Rook's. Bishops move along the diagonals of the chessboard. Look at Diagram 11.

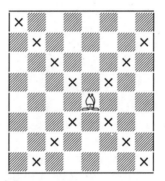

Diagram 11: How the Bishop moves

The White Bishop can move along the diagonals to any of the 13 squares indicated by the arrows. Notice two things about the Bishop's way of moving.

• A Bishop that starts on a white square will remain on white squares until the end of the game (and ditto for a black-squared Bishop).

• A Bishop travelling on squares of one color can never attack an enemy piece on a square of the other color.

17

This makes a Bishop a little less powerful than a Rook, since a Rook can eventually attack all the squares on the board, while a Bishop can only reach half the squares.

At the beginning of the game, each side has one Bishop that moves on White squares, and one Bishop that moves on dark squares. As long as a player keeps both his Bishops, they can together reach all the squares on the board.

Like the King and Rook, a Bishop can be blocked from moving by its own pieces, while it can capture an enemy piece on a square within its range. Look at Diagram 12.

Diagram 12: How the Bishop captures

The White Bishop can move up the board to the left and capture the Black Rook, or it can move down the board to the left and capture the Black Knight. It can't capture the Black Queen, because its own pawn prevents it from moving in that direction. It's also blocked from moving up to the right by its own King.

THE QUEEN
The Queen is the most powerful piece on the board. It combines the powers of the Rook and the Bishop, so it can travel up and down, left and right like the Rook, and also along the diagonals like the Bishop. Look at Diagram 13.

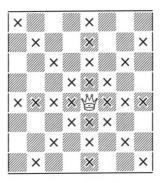

Diagram 13: How the Queen moves

The arrows show the squares to which the White Queen can move. If you count, you'll find that the Queen, from this open position, can reach 27 squares - that's almost half the squares on the board. Guard your Queen carefully. Her loss often means the loss of the game.

Although the Queen is the most powerful piece on the board, she can be restricted in her movements by her own pieces, just like the Rook and the Bishop. She can't leap over her own pieces to get to the enemy.

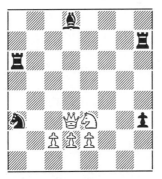

Diagram 14: How the Queen captures

In Diagram 14, the Queen is prevented from moving backwards by her own pawns, and from moving to the right by her Knight. She can't capture the Black pawn which lies beyond the Knight, however, she can capture any of the other four Black pieces by moving either straight ahead, to the left, or diagonally.

19

THE KNIGHT

The Knight is shaped like a horse's head, and is the most idiosyncratic of the pieces. Unlike the other pieces, the Knight cannot be blocked, either by its own pieces or the enemy's. It moves by hopping from square to square, and it hops over any pieces that are in the way. Look at Diagram 15.

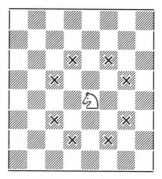

Diagram 15: How the Knight moves

In Diagram 15, the White Knight can move to any of the squares marked with an 'x'. You might want to think of its move as consisting of two moves: first a move of two squares either left, right, up, or down, then a move of one square at right angles to its first move. Another way is to think of it as one square left, right, up, or down, then one square diagonally away from its starting square. Use whatever method is easiest for you; you'll get used to the Knight's peculiar movement quickly enough.

Notice that if the Knight starts on a white square, it will end its turn on a black square, and vice-versa. If you move a Knight from a white square to another white square, you've made a mistake.

The Knight's ability to hop over other pieces on the way to its objective makes it a strong strategic piece. No barrier is secure against a Knight's attack. Look at Diagram 16.

Diagram 16: How the Knight captures

The Black Queen looks secure in the corner, guarded by an array of pieces and pawns. But the White Knight is able to leap over these men and capture the Queen. The position after the capture is shown in Diagram 17.

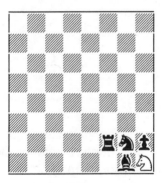

Diagram 17: The Knight has captured the Queen

Notice that the Knight didn't capture any of the pieces it jumped over. It only captured the piece occupying the square it landed on. That's very different from what happens in the game of checkers, where you capture the pieces you jump over. Remember that in chess, it's only the square you land on that matters.

THE PAWN
A pawn has the option of moving forward one or two squares on its very first move. After a pawn has moved, it can only move one square forward on subsequent moves.

Unlike the other pieces, a pawn may only move forwards, and never backwards. In Diagram 18, the pawn on the left of the diagram is still on the second rank, and therefore has the choice of moving forward one square or two (marked by x's in the diagram). The pawn in the center is beyond the second row, and so can only move forward to the square marked 'x'. The pawn on the right is blocked by the enemy pawn, and cannot move at all.

Now let's look at the pawn's movement more closely. See Diagram 18.

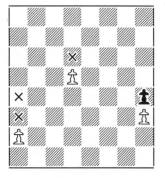

Diagram 18: How the pawn moves

Also, unlike the other pieces, pawns do not capture the same way they move. Pawns capture enemy pieces and pawns located diagonally in front of them. Look at Diagram 19.

Diagram 19: How the pawn captures.

The White pawn in Diagram 19 has a choice of three plays. It can move one square forward, to the black square in between the two Black pieces, or it can capture the Black Knight, or it can capture the Black Queen. The position after capturing the Black Queen is shown in Diagram 20.

Diagram 20: **After the pawn has captured the Queen**

PAWN PROMOTION

Now let's take a look at the pawn's special power - **pawn promotion.** A pawn that survives the rigors of battle and marches all the way to the eighth row of the board gets promoted to either a Queen, Rook, Bishop, or Knight, at your choosing. Often the promotion of a single pawn can be the decisive factor at the end of a long, close game.

Look at Diagram 21.

Diagram 21: **White to move**

White's pawn on the left side of the board has marched all the

23

way to the seventh rank. It's White's turn. White can move the pawn up one more square, to the last rank. Once it reaches the eighth rank, White gets to exchange it for any other piece, except the King. Usually, White chooses the Queen, since it's the most powerful piece. The position after White moves the pawn and promotes it is shown in Diagram 22.

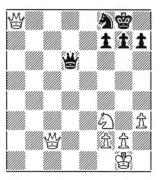

Diagram 22: White has promoted his pawn to a Queen

Note that pawn promotion is one move, not two. White simply picks up his pawn, pushes it one square, and then immediately replaces it with a White Queen. Then it's Black's turn.

Pawn promotion is not affected by the pieces remaining on the board. If White still has his original Queen (as he does in Diagram 22), he can promote a pawn and get a second Queen, and later on even a third. Some famous games have concluded with four Queens roaming around the board at the same time!

EN PASSANT

One special rule we need to learn about is called capturing **en passant**. It's a way of capturing a pawn with another pawn which may look peculiar at first. Take a look at Diagram 23.

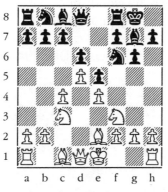

Diagram 23: Black to move

It's Black's move in Diagram 23. Suppose Black decides he wants to move the pawn to the left of his Queen. If he moves the pawn one square, it can be captured by the White pawn in the center of the board. But suppose he decides to move it two squares, bypassing the White pawn? Look at Diagram 24.

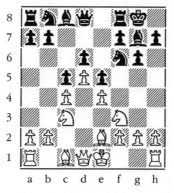

Diagram 24: Black has moved his pawn two squares

In this case, the White pawn in the center can capture the Black pawn *as if it had moved only one square*.

Capturing *en passant* can only be done by a pawn sitting on its fifth row to capture an enemy pawn on an adjacent file when that pawn advances two squares on its first move. This capture can only be performed on the very next turn. If White in Diagram 24 moved another piece, he would then lose the right to make that *en passant* capture at any future time.

The resulting position is shown in Diagram 25.

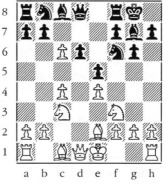

Diagram 25: White has captured en passant

CASTLING

There is one more rule we need to learn before we've completed the rules of movement - **castling**. Castling is a way of safeguarding the King, and it's the only move that involves moving two pieces at the same time.

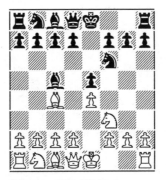

Diagram 26: White to move

Take a look at Diagram 26. We're on the fourth move of a game, and each side has moved a pawn, a Bishop, and a Knight. It's White's move. White, if he wants to, can now castle. Castling

26

is a move involving the King and the Rook, and it's done as follows:

KING-SIDE CASTLING

- Move the King two squares toward the Rook.
- Hop the Rook over the King.

The result is shown in the next diagram, number 27:

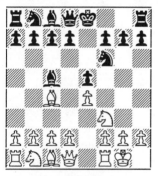

Diagram 27: White has castled King-side

Even though two pieces were involved, castling is considered a single move.

You might well ask at this point: "Why would you castle?" To answer that question, we're going to have to jump ahead a bit and delve into strategy and history.

The center of the board is the area where most of the early action in a chess game takes place. Experience shows that the King is safest in the corner of the board, while the Rooks belong in the center. Back in the late fifteenth century, most of the rules of chess were changed to their current form. Prior to that time, the Queens and Bishops were much weaker pieces than they are today, and the game developed more slowly.

After the rule changes, slashing attacks were possible right in the very opening, and the Kings were often caught in the center of the board. Castling was developed as a quick way to get the

King out of danger and the Rook into the thick of the action.

Black, of course, has the same right of castling as White. Diagram 28 shows what the board looks like if Black castles.

Diagram 28: Black has castled King-side

The castling we showed in Diagrams 27 and 28 is called **King-side castling**, because it occurs in the right-half of the chess board, where the Kings start at the beginning of the game. It's also possible to castle on the other side, which is called **Queen-side castling**. Take a look at Diagram 29.

Diagram 29: White to move

In Diagram 29, we see a position where both sides have developed all their pieces from the first rank except the Kings and the Rooks. Now the players are free to castle on the Queen-side. The rules for castling Queen-side are the same as the rules for castling King-side:

QUEEN-SIDE CASTLING

• Move the King two squares toward the Rook.
• Hop the Rook over the King.

The result after both White and Black have castled Queen-side is shown in Diagram 30:

Diagram 30: Both sides have castled Queen-side

That explains the **how** of castling, but what about the **when**? When is it legal to castle?

In order to castle, the following conditions have to be met:

(1) You must have no pieces between your King and the Rook. That means that, for King-side castling, you will have to have moved the Bishop and Knight that sit between the King and the Rook at the start of the game. For Queen-side castling, you will have to have moved not only the Bishop and Knight, but the Queen as well.

(2) The King must not have moved yet. Once the King has moved, you cannot castle on either side.

(3) The Rook with which you are castling must not have moved. But if you move one Rook, you still have the option

of castling with the other Rook.

(4) Your opponent must not control either the square that the King moves over or the square that the King lands on with one of his pieces. Thus, no opponent's piece may either occupy those squares, or hold those square in check.

(5) Your King must not be in check.

RELATIVE VALUE OF THE PIECES

In chess, it's possible to assign a numeric value to each of the pieces, as a way of evaluating exchanges and trades. Keep one fact firmly in mind, however. The list of relative values is solely for your own use during a game to help you evaluate the relative merit of exchanges of pieces. It has nothing to do with actually winning or losing the game. You don't win a chess game by accumulating points. You win by checkmating your opponent. In the next chapter, we'll see how to do that.

Take a look at this table:

Queen	9 points
Rook	5 points
Bishop	3 points
Knight	3 points
Pawn	1 point

The pawn is the least valuable piece, worth only 1 point. Next are the Bishop and Knight, at 3 points each. Bishops and Knights are sometimes known as **minor pieces**, to distinguish them from **major pieces**, the Rooks and Queen. Next comes the Rook, at 5 points. Most valuable of all is the Queen, at 9 points.

You can use this table to evaluate possible trades and exchanges. For instance, suppose you saw an opportunity to exchange a Bishop and a pawn for your opponent's Rook. You'd be giving up pieces worth 4 points for a Rook, worth 5 points. That's a good trade for you, about equivalent to winning a pawn outright.

Notice that the King isn't on this list, since he can't be traded for any other pieces. As a fighting piece, though his value is about equivalent to a Bishop or a Knight.

4. CHECK & CHECKMATE

Now that we've seen how to move the pieces, it's time to move on to the most important rules in chess - those covering "check" and "checkmate". It's these elements that determine how a game is won and lost.

As we said earlier, the King is the most important piece on the board and must never be allowed to be captured. Thus, when the King is attacked, you must first safeguard the King from capture before undertaking anything else.

To attack the enemy King, you simply move a piece or pawn to a square where it can capture the King on your next turn. When the King is so attacked, he is said to be *in check*. When you attack the enemy King, it's considered in good form to say "check", although this is not mandatory. What is mandatory, however, is that when you check your opponent's King, your opponent must remove his King from danger before doing anything else.

Look at Diagrams 31 and 32.

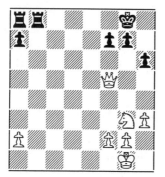

Diagram 31: Black to move

Diagram 32: Black checks

Diagram 31 shows a position with Black to move. Suppose Black picks up his Rook (the one on the dark square) and moves it all the way down the board to the first rank. The resulting position is shown in Diagram 32. Black announces "check".

Now it's White's turn. Take a close look at Diagram 32. Notice that the Black rook, by threatening to move horizontally along the first rank, is now in a position to capture the White King next turn. White's King is under attack, or "in check".

What can White do on his turn? Normally, when it's your turn, you have the option of moving any piece you want to any square it can reach. But when you're in check, that's no longer the case. When you're in check, you must make a move to get out of check.

There are three ways to get out of check. In Diagram 32, all three of these ways are available to White, although that won't be the case in most positions.

The first and simplest way to get out of check is to move the King to a position of safety. In Diagram 32, White has one move to do this: he can move the King one square up and to the right, to the vacant Black square. The resulting position is shown in Diagram 33.

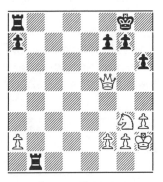

Diagram 33: White moves his King out of check

Notice that White couldn't have moved the King to either of the White squares on his left or right. From either of those squares, he would still have been under attack from the Black Rook. From its position, the Rook sweeps the whole first row, and keeps it off limits now to the White King. And of course, the King is blocked by his own pawns from moving to either of the other two squares on the second row.

The second way to get out of check is to block the Rook's check by interposing another piece between the Rook and the King. In Diagram 32, suppose that White picks up his Knight and hops it backwards, over his own pawns, to the white square to the left of the King. The resulting position is shown in Diagram 34.

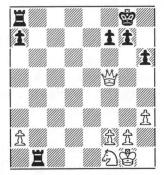

Diagram 34: White interposes his Knight

Now the Rook attacks the Knight, but not the King behind the

t effectively shields the King.

en most effective way of getting the King out of
ure the checking piece. In Diagram 32, White
ueen backwards along the white diagonal and
ck Rook. Diagram 35 shows the result.

Diagram 35: White captures the Rook

The Rook is no longer on the board, so the King is out of danger.

Even though it's not a requirement, it's a good idea to get in the habit of saying "check" whenever you attack your opponent's King. If he doesn't see the attack and makes another play, you don't win the game; you're obliged to point out that he's made an illegal move. He then has to retract the move he made and get his King out of check, instead.

Just because you can check your opponent doesn't mean you necessarily want to do so. If your opponent can defend against your check with a useful move (developing a piece, for instance), your check may be counter-productive. Always ask yourself: "Will this check inconvenience my opponent in some way?" If the answer is yes, then go ahead and check. If the answer is no, look for a better move. Another rule to be aware of: you can never move your King into check, of course.

"So, how do you win a game?" you might ask. That's done by administering checkmate. Let's take a look at some examples.

CHECKMATE

Checkmating your opponent is the goal of every chess game. The idea behind checkmate is simple: if you check your opponent, and he has **no legal way** to get out of check on the next turn, then he is **checkmated**, and the game is over. Let's look at a few examples of checkmates.

Let's go back to Diagram 31 and change the position somewhat. We'll interchange White's Queen and Knight, and move the pawn to the right of the King back one square. As we'll see, these small changes make a big difference.

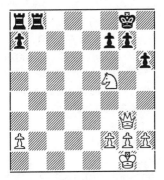

Diagram 36: Black to move

In Diagram 36, Black once again picks up his Rook and moves it down to the first rank, announcing "check". White must get out of check. But what are his options? Look at Diagram 37.

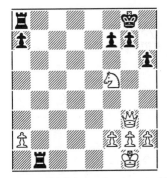

Diagram 37: Black has checkmated White

White can't move out of check. His King has only two available squares, on the left and the right, and those squares are both under attack by the Black rook. So moving the King won't save White.

Can White capture the Black Rook? No. The Knight is too far away, and the Queen is no longer in position to capture. Can White interpose a piece to block the check? Again, the answer is no - there's no piece in position to get back to the first row.

So White can't get out of check this turn - that's **checkmate**, and it means the game is over and Black has won.

Checkmate is the goal of every game. Both players try to maneuver their army into position to checkmate the opponent's King. The only other way to win a game is by concession; your opponent sees that checkmate is inevitable, and gives up rather than play on to a foregone conclusion. For now, however, leave concession to higher level players; play your games to a conclusion, and make your opponent checkmate you. It's not always so easy, and you may be able to save some games that look hopeless by tenacious defense.

Now let's look at some other examples of checkmate. Let's go back to Diagram 36, and suppose for a moment that it's White's turn to move, not Black's. Can you see how White can checkmate Black?

Here's the answer: White moves his Queen straight up the board and captures the pawn in front of Black's King.

See Diagram 38.

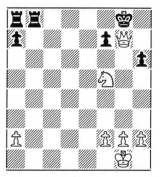

Diagram 38: White has checkmated Black

The White Queen now threatens to capture the Black King next turn, so White says "check". What are Black's options? He can't move out of check, since the three vacant squares around the King are also attacked by the Queen. (Don't forget, the Queen moves in all directions, diagonally as well as in straight lines.)

Black can't interpose a piece between the King and the Queen, since the Queen is right next to him. And Black can't capture the Queen with the King, since the Queen is "guarded" by the White Knight. (If the Black King captured the Queen, he would still be in check from the White Knight.) So the King is in check, with no way out - checkmate.

Let's look at one more example of checkmate.

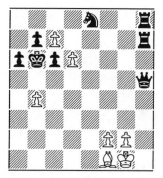

Diagram 39: White to move

White is clearly hurting in Diagram 39. Black has a Queen and two Rooks lined up on the right-hand side of the board, ready to swoop down and give checkmate. In fact, if it were Black's turn, he could move his Queen down into the white square in the lower right-hand corner of the board and announce "checkmate" right on the spot!

Fortunately for White, it's his turn to move. But what can he do? He only has a lone Bishop and a measly assortment of pawns to stem the tide. True, he could push his pawn that's now on the seventh rank up to the eighth rank and exchange it for a Queen, but so what? The Queen wouldn't be in a position to give check, and Black in his turn could simply administer the checkmate we pointed out before.

Although it looks hopeless at first glance, White has a hidden resource. If he sees it, he can checkmate Black this turn. Do you see how?

To figure out the solution, remember what we said a little while ago about pawn promotion. When you push a pawn to the eighth rank, you can exchange it for any piece, not just a Queen. Promoting to a Queen loses, as we saw, but suppose White promotes to a Knight! Look at Diagram 40.

Diagram 40: White has checkmated Black

White has promoted his pawn to a Knight, announcing "check" at the same time. What can Black do? The three open squares

40

in front of him are controlled by White's pawn and Bishop (don't forget the White Bishop, controlling the white diagonal). The other White pawn controls the square to the Black King's right rear. Three other squares are blocked by the Black pawn, impeding their King. The final square over in the left corner is also controlled by White's Knight. Black has no piece that can take the Knight. And finally, since a Knight can hop over obstacles, no piece can interpose against a Knight's check.

Study this checkmate carefully until you understand it completely. It's the most complicated play we've seen thus far.

In most chess games, checkmating your opponent is the culmination of a five-part strategy:

CHECKMATE STRATEGY

• Capture more of your opponent's pieces than he can capture of yours, so that you build up a solid material superiority.

• Exchange off your opponent's remaining pieces, so he is left with only his King and a few pawns.

• Use your extra material to shepherd a pawn to the Queening square.

• With your extra Queen, crowd your opponent's King to the edge of the board or into a corner, where its mobility is restricted.

• Checkmate him there.

This isn't the only way to do it, and sometimes checkmates will happen in the middle game or even in the opening itself. But the end of many chess games will follow this five-step process.

5. CHESS NOTATION

Up until now, we've described the position of the pieces and the moves of the game in a casual manner: "the pawn on the left side of the board", "the black square diagonally up from White's King", and so forth. This has worked so far because our positions have been simple, with just a few pieces and pawns on the board. It would quickly get cumbersome, however. We'd be saying things like "Move the pawn in front of the White Bishop that's next to the White King one square forward".

Fortunately, in chess, there's a simple, unambiguous way to describe moves and positions on the chessboard. It's called **standard chess notation**, and it's used all over the world to record and play back games, and also to write down chess positions. It's easy to learn, and once you know it, you'll not only be able to read chess books, you'll be able to play over games from the great tournaments and matches that are reported in the newspapers and the online services. Let's see how it works.

Chess notation starts by putting a coordinate grid over the chessboard.

Take a look at Diagram 41.

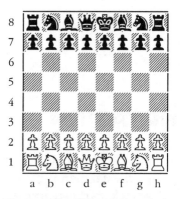

Diagram 41: The notation system

Notice that we've added letters and numbers around the edge of the board. The horizontal rows, or **ranks**, have been numbered from 1 to 8. White's first row, the rank containing the White pieces, is number 1. The rank with Black's pieces is now number 8. The vertical rows, or **files**, are lettered **"a"** through **"h"**, with "a" starting on White's left and "h" on White's right.

This grid system lets us refer to any square on the board by a unique name. White's King is currently sitting on the square "e1". Black's Queen is on square "d8", and so on.

In addition to the grid system, we have abbreviations for each of the pieces. Here they are:

ABBREVIATIONS FOR THE PIECES	
King	K
Queen	Q
Rook	R
Bishop	B
Knight	N
Pawn	-

To indicate a move, we write down the piece that moved, and the starting and ending squares of the move. However, if a pawn is moving, we don't write anything more than the starting and ending squares.

We use a dash to separate the starting and ending squares, and an "x" if the move was a capture.

Now let's play through the first few moves of a sample game. If you can follow along, you've got the hang of it.

	White	Black
1	e2-e4	...

Notice that we write the moves in columns. White's column comes first, then Black's. White's first move is e2 to e4. Since no piece is indicated, White has moved a pawn. Move the pawn on the e2 square two spaces forward, to the e4 square. Your board should look like this:

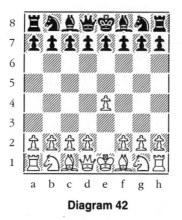

Diagram 42

The game continues:

1	...	e7-e5
2	Ng1-f3	Nb8-c6

Black then moved the pawn in front of his King two squares, from e7 to e5. White moved his King-side Knight from the g1 square to the f3 square. And Black responded by playing his Knight from b8 to c6. You should now have this position on your board:

45

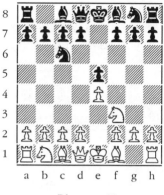

Diagram 43

Let's play along a few more moves.

3	Bf1-b5	a7-a6
4	Bb5xc6	d7xc6
5	d2-d3	Bc8-g4

If your board now looks like the next diagram, you've mastered chess notation!

Diagram 44

SPECIAL NOTATIONS

Certain moves in chess have their own special notation.

• Castling King-side is denoted by "0-0". Castling Queen-side is denoted by "0-0-0".

• When promoting a pawn, indicate the promoted piece in parentheses: for instance, "a7-a8 (Q)" says that White moved a pawn to the a8 square and promoted it to a Queen.

• Capturing *en passant* is indicated by "ep" after the move: for instance, "d5xc6 ep" shows a pawn capturing *en passant* on the c6 square.

There's one other aspect of chess notation. We use exclamation points and question marks to comment on the ingenuity or effectiveness of moves.

Here's what they mean:

! means a good move.

!! means a brilliant, completely unexpected move.

? means an error.

?? means a gross blunder, probably losing the game.

---

6. DRAWN GAMES

Not all chess games end in victory for one side. It's possible for neither side to win. That's called a **drawn game**. In tournaments, a player scores one point when he wins a game, but nothing if he loses. In the case of a drawn game, each player scores half a point.

There are several ways a game can end in a draw. The simplest is when the players reach a position where neither side can checkmate the other. Suppose, for instance, the players trade off all the pieces until each is left with only a King. In that case, neither player can even check the other since the King is not allowed to move into check, let alone give checkmate. So the game would be abandoned as a draw.

Another example would be a position where one side has a King and Bishop, while the other side has only a King. While the King and Bishop would be able to check the enemy King from time to time, they could never control enough squares to give checkmate. (Try this yourself on an empty board to verify that it can't be done.) In the same way, King and Knight versus King is also a drawn endgame.

King and pawn vs. King, however, is often a winning advantage. If the pawn is in position to be promoted to a Queen, the resulting Queen and King will easily be able to checkmate the lone King.

STALEMATE

Another example of a drawn game is what's called a **stalemate**. This is when one side is not currently in check but cannot make a move without moving into check! Take a look at Diagram 45.

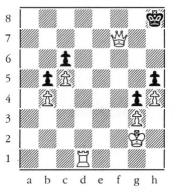

Diagram 45: Black is stalemated

It's Black's move. But Black doesn't have a legal move. All his pawns are blocked and can't advance, and his King can't move without moving into check from the White Queen. However, the position is not a checkmate, since Black is not currently in check! This is called a stalemate, and the game is scored as a draw, no matter how far ahead in material one side may be.

CHECKMATE AND STALEMATE

Be aware of the difference between checkmate and stalemate:

• If you're in **check**, and you don't have a way to get out of check, that's **checkmate**, and you lose.

• If you're not in check, but you can't move without moving into check, that's **stalemate**, and the game is a draw.

Stalemate is a powerful resource. Many seemingly hopeless games have been saved when one side discovered a stalemate defense.

PERPETUAL CHECK

Another type of drawn game results when the players get into a situation known as **perpetual check**. Take a look at the next diagram:

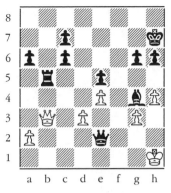

Diagram 46: White to move

White is in a very bad way, apparently at the verge of defeat. Black has an extra Bishop and Rook, plus a few spare pawns. Some players might give up in White's position, but White finds a way to save the game.

He starts by playing Qb3-f7 check! Black can only get out of check by moving his King, and he has only one square to move to: h8. So he plays Kh7-h8. Now White plays Qf7-f8 check! Black has to go back to h7. Then White plays Qf8-f7 check! Get the idea? Black would like to stop the checks, but he can't. But if White stops giving check, he will quickly be mated. White announces that he intends to continue giving check, and the result is that the game is a draw, since neither side can now win.

OTHER DRAWN GAMES
Two other ways of drawing a game are unusual and are rarely seen outside of formal tournaments.

The first is called **triple repitition**: if the same position occurs three times in a game with the same player on move, the player on move can declare the game a draw. The second is known as the **fifty-move rule**: if fifty moves go by without a capture or a pawn move, either player can declare the game a draw.

A final way of drawing the game is for the combatants to shake hands and agree to a draw. Don't worry about that for now. Leave the agreed draws to the grandmasters and concentrate on beating your opponent!

7. GENERAL WINNING STRATEGY

So far, we've learned about the **elements** of chess - how the pieces move, how to checkmate the opposing King, how to write down moves in chess notation, and how a game can end in a draw. Now it's time to move on to the next question: How does one go about winning a chess game? What should I be thinking about while I'm playing?

Broadly speaking, advice about how to make good moves in chess can be broken into two categories: strategy and tactics.

Strategy is the big picture: strategic rules tell us how to develop our pieces, what parts of the board are most important, and how to plan our campaign. Strategic rules in chess are analogous to strategic rules of warfare - rules like "Control the air", "Seize the high ground", and "Direct your attack at the enemy's weakest point."

Tactics is the little picture: tactical rules tell us how to win a game at the micro level. They're analogous to rules of hand-to-hand combat on the battlefield. By mastering the principles of tactics, we learn how to capture more of our opponent's pieces and pawns than he can capture of ours.

Which part of the game is more important? Both work together in unison, but make no mistake - chess is 90% tactics. A great strategical plan is worthless if your opponent picks off your Queen in the middle of it.

OPENING, MIDDLE AND ENDGAME OVERVIEW

Let's step back a moment and look at the overall development of a typical chess game. In general, most games can be divided into three distinct phases: the **opening**, the **middle game**, and the **endgame**. Each phase has distinct goals and objectives.

- In the **opening**, strive for quick and harmonious development. Get your pieces out and safeguard your King. In most games, the opening is finished by moves 10-15, although in well-studied openings, it might last even longer.

- In the **middle game**, coordinate your pieces and attack your opponent's weak spots. The objective is to win material, or in some cases, checkmate the opponent's King. In the middle game, tactics predominate. The middle game extends from the end of the opening to move 40 or so.

- In the **endgame**, use your remaining pieces to exploit the advantages you won in the middle game. The endgame often concludes with one side shepherding a pawn through to the Queening square, followed by a checkmate or resignation. Although tactics play a role in the endgame, strategy is predominant here.

OPENING GAME STRATEGY

What's our main goal in the opening? Answer: **Control the center**. What do we mean by the center?

Take a look at the next diagram.

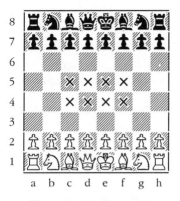

Diagram 47: The center

Notice the block of squares in the middle of the board marked with x's. That's what we call the **center**, and it's the most important part of the chessboard. Pieces placed in the center of the board have the greatest power of movement. They're in position to move to the King-side or the Queen-side, attack or retreat, as required by the situation.

Pieces on the edge of the board, on the other hand, have much less scope for attack. They don't influence the center as much, and they can't be quickly transferred from one side to the other.

At the start of the game, all your pieces are on the edge of the board! That's not where they want to be. You want to be maneuvering them into positions of influence in the center as quickly as possible. To do that, you need to move the pawns that are currently blocking their progress. There are two good moves to start this process along - e2-e4 and d2-d4. Either one places a pawn right in the center of the board and opens lines for the Queen and a Bishop.

In the opening, we control the center by **developing** pieces; that is, moving pieces off the back rank and into battle. That should be a key goal of your opening strategy: develop your pieces, preferably toward the center of the board, and mobilize them for the coming fight.

In what order should you develop your pieces in the opening? Experience shows that the following plan works well:

ORDER OF OPENING DEVELOPMENT

• Start with either the King and Queen pawns, moving them two spaces forward to grab some center space.

• Next come the Knights, to f3 and c3 for White, f6 and c6 for Black.

• Next come the Bishops, to whatever squares on the diagonals that seem useful under the circumstances.

• Castle the King, to get him safely into a corner.

• Finally bring out the most valuable pieces, the Rooks and the Queen, but not too far from home.

What's wrong with developing the Queen early in the opening? The reason is simple. Your Queen is your most powerful, but also (next to the King) your most important piece. If she goes out into the fray early, she'll probably get attacked by your opponent's less-valuable Knights, Bishops, and pawns. Faced with those attacks, she'll have to retreat. You can't afford to lose your Queen for, let's say, an enemy Knight.

Those retreats will mean a loss of time and position. Your opponent will be developing his game when you should be bringing other pieces into the fray.

Remember the original **Star Trek** show? Captain Kirk was always the first to beam down to a strange planet, at which point the primitive mugwumps would bash him on the head, steal his communicator, and throw him in a dungeon. The crew spent the rest of the show trying to get him out. On the new show, Captain Picard is smarter. He stays on the Enterprise coordinating things while Riker, Geordie, and Data get their heads bashed. Moral: let the expendable peons carve out unexplored territory. Your most important pieces should follow the shock troops into battle, not lead them.

That's the essence of strategy in the early part of the game: mobilize your pieces, control the center, and provide for the safety of the King and Queen. After both players have done that, the hand-to-hand fighting starts, and that's the arena of the middle game.

The opening is important because the tone and structure of the coming struggle is determined here. The amount of study and attention that's been devoted to chess openings is amazing. Professional players spend much of their time preparing new twists in the opening for their upcoming matches.

In our companion book, **Winning Chess Openings**, we'll show you how to get a winning advantage in the opening. You'll learn about the workhorse openings that form the bulk of most player's repertoire, like the King's Gambit, the Ruy Lopez, and the Queen's Gambit. You'll also learn about some of the offbeat openings that players sometimes adopt for surprise value, like the swashbuckling Evans' Gambit, the ancient Giuoco Piano Opening, and the wildly complex King's Indian Defense.

THE MIDDLE GAME - TACTICS
After the opening comes the middle game, where the real battles take place. Your goal in the middle game is more simple and straightforward: capture more of your opponent's pieces than he can capture of yours. The art of maneuvering and capturing in the middle game is called **Tactics**, and that's what we'll look at next.

Tactics is about winning your opponent's pieces for nothing, or for pieces of lesser value.

Remember our scale of the relative value of the pieces? The Queen was the most valuable piece, followed by the Rooks, then the Bishops and Knights, and finally the pawns.

If you can capture a more valuable piece (say a Rook) and give up something less valuable in return (say a pawn), you've made substantial progress toward winning the game. The reason is that your army now has more firepower than your opponent's. You can control more squares, and make more threats.

In time, as your advantage grows greater and greater, you may be able to force the win of still more material. Then your advantage is even greater. In time, your advantage may be large enough to be able to checkmate the enemy King himself.

Sometimes, particularly in games between beginners, you don't need to do anything special to win material: your opponent may just give it to you if you're alert enough to spot it. Consider the first three moves of this game:

	White:	Black:
1	e2-e4	e7-e5
2	Ng1-f3	Qd8-g5
3	Nf3xg5	

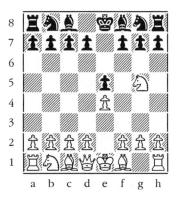

Diagram 48: White has captured Black's Queen

That was easy. Black didn't notice that White's Knight was guarding the square g5. Black put his Queen there, and White took it off. With an extra Queen, White should be able to win this game eventually.

However, it won't always be that easy. Many of your opponents will see your most obvious threats, and avoid placing their pieces where you can easily capture them. When playing such an opponent, you'll need to raise your game to a higher level. That's where **tactics** come in. In the rest of this chapter, we'll show you some tactical maneuvers that will make winning material much easier. Master these themes, and you'll make life very difficult for your opponent.

THE PIN

The first theme is the **pin**. Pins occur when you attack a less valuable piece which must stay where it is to guard a more valuable piece. Look at Diagram 49:

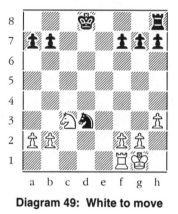

Diagram 49: White to move

In this position, the material is even: each side has a Rook, a Knight, and five pawns. The game looks equal. But White sees an opportunity to execute a **pin.** He moves his Rook from f1 to d1, attacking the Black Knight.

Look at the next diagram.

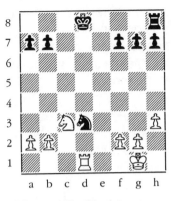

Diagram 50: Black to move

Normally Black would just move his Knight away from the Rook's attack. But here, he can't do that! If he moves his Knight, his King, located behind the Knight on the d-file, would be in check from the White Rook. The rules of chess are clear: you can't make a move that leaves your King in check. Black will have to leave his Knight where it is. Next turn White will play Rd1xd3, and he will be a Knight ahead, leaving him well on the way to victory.

Pins are common in chess and a player must be constantly alert for them.

THE FORK
Another tactical theme is the **Knight fork**, an often deadly maneuver!

Look at Diagram 51:

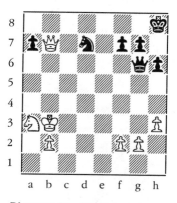

Diagram 51: Black to move

As in the previous example, material is even, both sides having a Queen, a Knight, and a few pawns. But not for long. Black, on move, sees a chance for a devastating Knight fork, and plays Nd7-c5 check! Take a look.

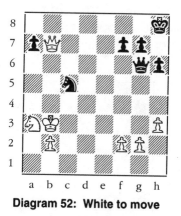

Diagram 52: White to move

The Knight is now attacking White's King. White has no choice: he must move his King somewhere, to get it out of check. But notice that the Knight is also attacking White's Queen! After White moves his King, Black will play Nc5xb7, winning White's Queen for nothing. The rest should be easy.

A fork is one example of a **double attack**, a move which attacks

61

two pieces at the same time. The double attack is the essence of successful tactical play. Since the defender can usually guard only one of the two pieces, the other piece is lost. Take a look at the next diagram.

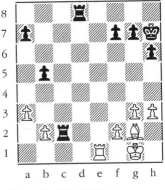

Diagram 53: White to move

White is losing in Diagram 53. His Bishop and Rook are worth a little less than Black's two Rooks. But White can save himself with a tactical resource, a **double attack**. He moves his Bishop from g2 to e4, announcing check.

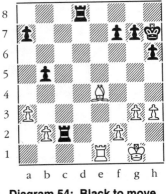

Diagram 54: Black to move

The Bishop attacks two Black pieces, the King and the Rook. Black has no choice - he must move his King out of check. Next turn, White will snap up the Rook, leaving himself a Bishop to the good.

DISCOVERED ATTACKS

In chess, pieces can make direct threats themselves, but by moving they may also uncover threats from the pieces behind them. These are called **discovered attacks**. Stay alert to them.

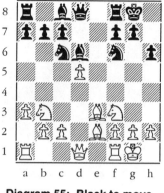

Diagram 55: Black to move

Take a look at Diagram 55. White is quite happy with his position. He is a pawn ahead, and he has just pushed his pawn from d4 to d5, attacking Black's Knight at c6. Black will, he imagines, move his attacked Knight back somewhere, after which White can continue with a move like c2-c4, gaining ground in the center. Very nice, says White.

But Black has a surprise: he plays instead Nf6xd5! Take a look.

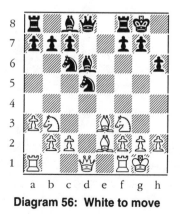

Diagram 56: White to move

"What's this?" says White to himself. "Black has captured my pawn. Obviously he doesn't notice my Queen on d1, defending the pawn. Foolish fellow. I will capture his Knight, leaving me a piece ahead. This game will be easier than I thought." White plays Qd1xd5.

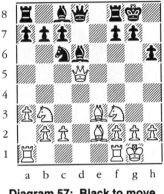

Diagram 57: Black to move

But Black knew what he was doing, and now he springs his trap. He plays Bd6xh2 check!

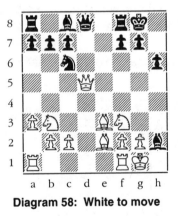

Diagram 58: White to move

Black moves his Bishop, attacking White's King. White can take the Bishop with either his Knight on f3 or his King. But look: the Bishop, by moving, has uncovered an attack on the White Queen by the Black Queen on d8. No matter how White gets out of check, Black's next move will be Qd8xd5, and Black will have won a Queen while losing a Bishop and a Knight - a very favorable trade for him.

These are just a few of the tactical motifs of chess. Learn them, and try to recognize such opportunities in your games. By mastering these ideas, you'll find you have a big edge over most of your opponents!

THE ENDGAME
The endgame is the time when the material advantage built up in the middle game is translated into checkmate. Usually this is done by trading off the remaining pieces (to prevent the defender from putting up any real resistance), marching a pawn down the board and Queening it, and then administering checkmate with overwhelming force.

The second sample game in this book concludes with a textbook example of this process.

8. SAMPLE GAME - DEVELOPMENT STRATEGY

PREVIEW

Now we're ready to take a look at an actual game, so get out your chessboard, set it up in the beginning position, (Diagram 2), and follow along with us. It's important that you make the moves on your chessboard as we describe them here in the book. That way you'll get used to moving actual pieces around an actual board.

Let's meet our two players. White is a relative novice, with a few games under his belt, but not much knowledge of strategy. For a novice, however, White is relatively good at spotting direct threats and defending against them. Black is a much more experienced player, with a couple of years' experience and a good grasp of both strategy and tactics. (As the game goes on, I'll explain more clearly what I mean by these terms.)

The moves of the game are given in two columns. White's moves are in the first column, followed by Black's moves in the second column. The moves are also numbered, so later we can easily refer back to moves that happened earlier in the game.

Is your board set up? Good. Let's go!

THE GAME

	White	Black
1	d2-d3	

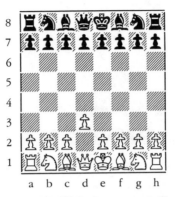

Diagram 59: White has moved d2-d3

White begins the game by moving the pawn in front of his Queen one square forward. That's not a particularly good way to open the game: better moves, for example, are e2-e4 or d2-d4, moving the pawns in front of the King or Queen two squares forward.

What's wrong with White's actual play of d2-d3? For one thing, the pawn is less influential on d3 than it would be on d4. There's another reason, but it's a bit more subtle. Although moving the pawn to d3 opens up a diagonal for the Bishop on c1, it closes a diagonal for the Bishop on f1. The White-squared Bishop used to be blocked on the diagonal from f1 to a6 by one pawn, the pawn on e2. Now it's blocked by two pawns: those on e2 and d3. In the opening of the game, it's important to open up lines for your pieces, not to block them in.

| 1 | ... | e7-e5 |

(The three dots in White's column indicates that we've already seen White's first move, and now we're looking at Black's move.)

Black, on his part, makes an excellent first move. He advances the King's pawn two squares, immediately attacking the squares f4 and d4. At the same, Black's Queen and King's Bishop now have open diagonals to move upon. Black couldn't accomplish more with one move.

2   f2-f3   Ng8-f6

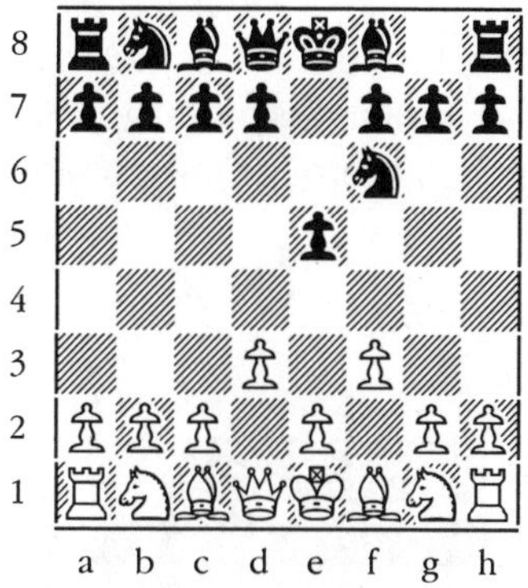

Diagram 60

WHITE ERRORS & BLACK RESPONSE

White's second move, f2-f3, was a more serious error than his first move. It didn't accomplish anything positive, and it hurt White's position in three ways:

• The pawn on f3 prevents White's Knight from moving to that square. In general, you want to get your Knights into the game early. The best squares for White's Knights are f3 and c3, while the best squares for Black's Knights are f6 and c6.

• The pawn on f3 creates an additional block for the White Queen along the diagonal running from d1 to h5. In the opening, you want to enhance the movement of your pieces, not restrict them.

• Moving the pawn from f2 to f3 opens a diagonal leading to White's King: the diagonal from e1 to h4. That's not a good idea. The King is the one piece whose loss will cost you the game, so you want to keep your King's position very secure. In practice, that means your King wants to sit somewhere safe and secure behind a wall of pawns. Moving pawns around your King makes it easier for your opponent to get at him.

Black's second move, the Knight from g8 to f6, was quite good. It **develops** a piece; that is, it moves a piece off the back rank and into battle. That should be a key goal of your opening strategy: develop your pieces, preferably toward the center of the board, and mobilize them for the coming fight.

3	h2-h4	Bf8-c5

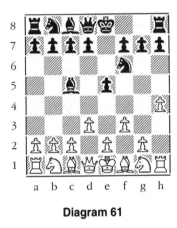

Diagram 61

White's third move is another error. He moves a pawn along the edge of the board, rather than contest the center with a move like e2-e4. True, his move gives some additional scope to his King's Rook. But the new squares that the Rook can reach (h2 and h3) are far removed from the center of the board, where the action will be.

Why is White playing this way? Actually, it's not at all uncommon for novices to start their first few games with moves like d2-d3 and h2-h4, especially if they haven't been instructed otherwise. To a beginner, a move like d2-d3 looks good because the pawn is close to home and securely protected. After all, on d3 the pawn is guarded by the pawns at c2 and e2, and also by the

White queen.

Similarly, the pawn on h4 is both guarded by the White Rook and well away from Black's pieces. These moves seem good to a beginner because they **look safe**. And a beginner, most of all, is concerned with protecting his pieces. Beginners don't put their pieces in the center because pieces there are exposed to attack.

However, this is quite wrong! In chess, *victory goes to the side with the most space and mobility.* Remember that. Fighting for the center isn't an option, it's a necessity.

DEVELOPING THE CENTER
Black's third move, Bishop to c5, was quite good. He developed a piece to an active position and seized control of more central squares.

4   Ng1-h3   ...

White's fourth move puts the Knight on a square at the edge of the board, not the most useful spot for it. Unfortunately, the square f3, the best square for the Knight in the opening, is now blocked by a White pawn.

Knights have a limited range compared to the Bishops and the Rooks, which can sweep across the whole board in one move. Therefore, it's especially important to get them into the game early. Although h3 doesn't bear on the important central squares, the move at least gets the Knight off the first rank and out into the game.

4   ...   d7-d5

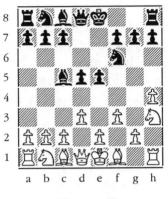

Diagram 62

Excellent! By advancing his Queen's pawn, Black takes over complete control of the central squares. The pawn occupies the d5 square, attacks the squares e4 and c4, preventing White from stationing pieces there, and opens up new lines of movement for the Queen and the Bishop on c8. It's hard to ask more of one simple move.

> 5   a2-a4   ...

White continues playing "safely", moving a pawn on the edge of the board. This strategy can only work for a few moves. Eventually, Black's preponderance of power in the center will begin to generate real threats, and White will have to mobilize to meet those threats. With his pieces scattered on the edges of the board, that will be hard to do.

> 5   ...   d5-d4

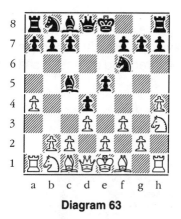

Diagram 63

Black pushes his Queen's pawn up another square and grabs more space in the center. The move has another point as well. Remember we said that in the openings, the best places for White's Knights were on the squares c3 and f3. By playing d5-d4, Black's pawn now attacks the c3 square, preventing White's Knight from moving there.

(It doesn't really **prevent** the move Nb1-c3, of course. White can legally put his Knight on the c3 square. But if he does, Black will capture it with his pawn. White would lose his Knight and get only a pawn in return, a highly unfavorable exchange for him. Remember that in our table of relative values of the pieces, a Knight was worth 3 points and a pawn only 1. In chess, that's often what we mean when we say a move is **prevented**: White could do it, but he would lose material as a result, so he shouldn't do it.)

Notice how Black's pawn moves in the center are gradually restricting White's options. His Knight on b1 can't go to c3, because a Black pawn guards that square. Similarly, his Knight on h3 can't go to f4; another Black pawn guards that square. His Bishop on c1 can't move to either e3 or f4 because of the Black pawns. As White's options shrink, good moves become harder and harder to find.

6   Qd1-d2   ...

White develops a piece, but the wrong piece. He would have been better off playing his Knight from b1 to d2, or pushing his pawn from c2 to c4, grabbing at least a share of the center.

6   ...   Nb8-c6

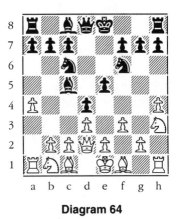

Diagram 64

Another good move, developing the Queen's Knight to a useful square. Black isn't trying at this point to do anything spectacular or brilliant. He's content to develop his pieces, certain that his superior development will eventually allow him to capitalize on White's more disorganized position.

7   Ra1-a2   ...

White's trying to develop, but it's difficult because Black controls so much of the center. If White moves the Rook farther into the game, by playing Ra1-a3, Black will be able to capture the Rook with the Bishop at c5. That's an advantageous exchange for Black: remember that Rooks are worth 5 points, Bishops only 3. White sees that possibility, and stops at the a2 square.

Still, it's too soon to be bringing the Rooks into play. A better idea

74

would be to develop the Knight from b1 to a3, with the idea next turn of swinging it over to c4. A Knight on c4 would exert some real influence on the central squares.

BLACK CONTINUES DEVELOPING

7	...	Bc8-e6

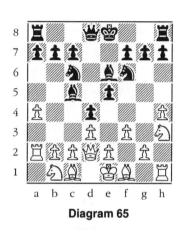

Diagram 65

Another fine move by Black. He develops, and with a threat as well. Take a close look at Diagram 65.

The Black Bishop on e6 now threatens to swoop down next turn and capture the White Rook on a2. That would be a huge advantage for Black; he'd pick up a whole Rook for nothing. White on his 8th move will have to try and prevent that in some way.

This is the basic way chess games are won, at least at the novice or beginner level. **Attack your opponent's pieces!** If he overlooks your attack, take his pieces off. Later, after you've established an overwhelming superiority in pieces, concentrate on checkmating the King.

8	b2-b3	...

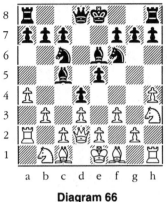

Diagram 66

White sees the threat and saves his Rook by blocking the Bishop's line of attack with a pawn. If Black captures the pawn with his Bishop, White will recapture with his pawn on c2, gaining a Bishop for a pawn. So Black won't capture.

What else could White do? As we saw last turn, he can't move his Rook forward to a3, because the Black Bishop on c5 could capture it there. He could move the Rook back to a1, but that would be a pretty ignominious retreat.

White had another possibility: he could have blocked the Bishop's attack by playing c2-c4 with his pawn. However, that would only have worked temporarily, because Black could respond with d4xc3 ep (*en passant*) - his pawn on d4 could move to c3, capturing the White pawn on c4 en passant! The Black pawn on c3 would then attack the White Queen on d2, while the Black Bishop on e6 would still be attacking the White Rook. That sequence would be a disaster for White.

8   ...   Nf6-d5

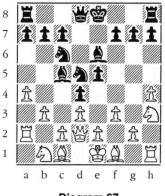

Diagram 67

Black moves his Knight to the center of the board. From d5, it threatens to penetrate further into White's position, to squares like e3 and c3.

The Knight's move has another point, however. Do you see it?

Take a look at the Black Queen. By moving the Knight, Black has opened the diagonal from d8 to h4 for the Black Queen. The Queen is now threatening to move to h4, capturing the White pawn and, incidentally, giving check to the White King.

In chess, pieces can make direct threats themselves, but by moving they may also uncover threats from the pieces behind them. These are called **discovered attacks**. Stay alert to them.

9   g2-g3   ...

White tries to do the best he can under the circumstances. He sees the threat to his h4 pawn (many novices would have overlooked this) and guards the pawn with another pawn, at the same time opening a square (g2) for his Bishop on f1. Given sufficient time, White might be able to play his Bishop to g2, castle with his King's Rook, and gradually mobilize his cramped army.

Black doesn't want to permit this. He now has complete control of the center of the board, and rather than slowly develop the rest of his army, decides to launch an immediate attack on White's position. Let's see how he does this.

BLACK BEGINS THE ATTACK

9   ...   Bc5-b4

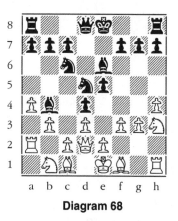

Diagram 68

Very good. Black finds a strong move. His Bishop attacks the White Queen. Why is this so strong? Because the Queen is guarding the King from attack. White would normally respond to the Bishop's attack by moving the Queen away, perhaps to g5 or d1. But here, moving the Queen would leave the King in check from the Black Bishop. This is an example of the tactical idea of the **pin**, which we discussed in Chapter 7.

Remember the two rules regarding check.

• If in check, you must get your King out of check before doing anything else.

• You must never move your King into check.

So White has a problem. He wants to save his Queen, but moving it away is illegal.

The Queen could capture the Bishop, but it would then be captured by one of the Black Knights. Not a good trade for White. He finds the only way to save his Queen.

10   c2-c3   ...

White blocks the Bishop's attack with his pawn, saving the Queen.

THE FIRST CAPTURE IS MADE

10   ...   Nd5xc3

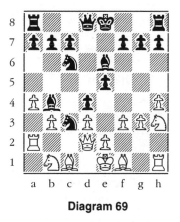

Diagram 69

Black captures the White pawn, the first capture of the game.

White can now capture the Black Knight with his Knight at b1 (Nb1xc3), but that would be a big mistake. Black would reply by capturing the Knight with his Bishop (Bb4xc3) and White's Queen would again be pinned against his King, this time with no escape. White would inevitably lose his Queen for the Black Bishop. White needs to find another way to save his Queen.

11   Ke1-f2   ...

White solves the problem by moving his King to the only

available square. (The King couldn't go to d1 because the Black Knight attacks that square.) With the King out of the way, the Queen is now free to move from the attack of the Black Bishop.

11   ...   Be6xb3

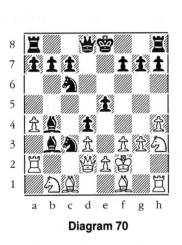

Diagram 70

The Bishop swoops down and captures the White pawn on b3, whose defender (the pawn on c2) was removed last turn. The Bishop now threatens the White Rook.

Notice how Black's early command of the center has been converted into a withering attack on the disorganized White position. White now has to scramble to save what he can.

12   Bc1-b2   ...

White moves the Bishop off the first rank to attack the Black Knight. A little better was Ra2-b2, leaving the Bishop where it was but saving the Rook.

DISCOVERED ATTACK!

12   ...   Nc3xb1

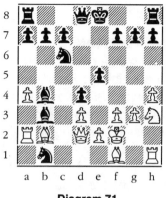

Diagram 71

Black disdains capturing the Rook and instead captures the White Knight. Also, here's another example of **discovered attack** that we saw on move 8: the Black Knight has uncovered an attack on the White Queen by the Black Bishop on b4. White will need to save his Queen before he can try to rescue the White Rook.

13   Qd2-c1   ...

The White Queen moves out of the Bishop's attack and in turn threatens the Black Knight.

13   ...   Bb3xa2

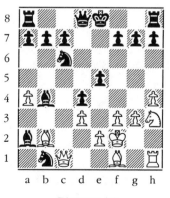

Diagram 72

The Bishop captures the White Rook, and at the same time defends the Black Knight from capture by the White Queen.

EVALUATING THE POSITION

The battle on the Queen side has temporarily come to an end. Black has captured a Knight, a Rook, and two pawns, while losing nothing of his own. White was undone by the awkward position of his pieces and the vulnerability of his King and Queen. White had to lose time saving his major pieces while the minor pieces were picked off.

Does White still have a chance to save the game?

Among strong players, the answer would be no. Good players are able to nurse an advantage of an extra Knight or Bishop along to victory without too much trouble. Among grandmasters, even the advantage of an extra pawn can be enough to win!

Among beginners, it's not so clear. Often, in games between novices, the advantage ebbs and flows between the two players. We shall see in a moment whether that's the case here. At any rate, White has nothing to lose by playing on and seeing what happens.

PLAYING ON

14   Bf1-g2   ...

White moves his Bishop off the first rank, opening a line for his Rook on h1 to enter the game. It's a modest beginning, but at this point any development is worthwhile.

14   ...   0-0

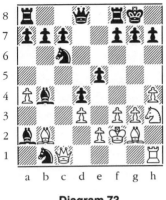

Diagram 73

Black castles on the King-side, moving his King into relative safety in the corner, while bringing the Rook closer to the scene of the action, the center.

15   Qc1-c2

White's move contains a threat, his first of the game. By moving the Queen, White uncovers an attack on the Black Knight by the Rook on h1. Although the Knight is protected by the Bishop, it is also attacked by the Queen. That's a total of two attackers and only one defender. White's threat is to play Rh1xb1. After Black replies Ba2xb1, White will finally capture with the Queen, Qc2xb1. The end result will be that Black will lose his Knight and his Bishop, while White will lose only a Rook in return. Since a Bishop and Knight are together worth 6 points, while a Rook is only worth 5, White will have made a small profit on the trade.

15   ...   Nb1-d2

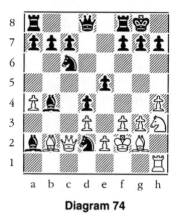

Diagram 74

The Knight steps aside and avoids the Rook's attack. The Knight is protected from capture by the Bishop at b4. Meanwhile, at d2 the Knight is closer to the White King, to assist in a possible later attack.

16   Qc2-d1   ...

It's not really clear what White intends by this move. On the other hand, the Queen had little scope where she was. Except for c1 and c2, all the other squares on the c-file are controlled by Black pieces. The Bishop on b4 guards c3 and c5, the Bishop on a2 guards c4, and the Knight on c6 is securely protected by the pawn on b7. With nowhere to go on the Queenside, it's not unreasonable for White to move the Queen over to the Kingside, where action may be brewing in the near future.

16   ...   Qd8-d7

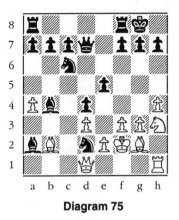

Diagram 75

THE QUEEN AND THE CANTER

Black also moves the Queen one square, but notice the difference! The Black Queen moves on to a new, more active diagonal, where she can observe the squares f5, g4, and h3. By moving off the eighth rank, she clears the way for the Rook at a8 to enter the game. In addition, she provides support for a future pawn advance by f7-f5.

The difference between White's Queen move and Black's is a function of the huge difference in controlled space. Black, with his pawns at d4 and e5 and his active minor pieces deep in White's position, controls most of the board. While White is reduced to creeping around on his first and second ranks, Black has the option of launching an attack on the Queenside, with moves like Ba2-b3, Nc6-a5, and Qd7xa4, or on the Kingside with moves like Ra8-e8, f7-f5, and e5-e4.

We can now see very clearly the consequences of losing the battle for the central squares.

WHITE GETS AGGRESSIVE

17   f3-f4   ...

An aggressive move. White is unwilling to passively sit back and be slowly crushed, so he makes a bid for more influence in the center. If Black takes the pawn by e5xf4, White can recapture with his Knight (Nh3xf4). At the same time, his Bishop on g2 now has more scope along the diagonal from g2 to c6.

There's a downside to this move as well, however. The pawn at f3 is currently guarding the White King against a future attack. Opening up the Kingside means opening up the lines of attack which point directly to the White King. However, it's too late to worry about this very much. White is losing and has to try to get something going, however dangerous it may be in the long run.

17 ...   f7-f6

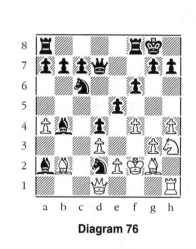

Diagram 76

Black supports the pawn on e5. Notice what would happen now if White captures by f4xe5. Black would respond with f6xe5, check! The White King would be in check, not from the Black pawn which moved, but from the Rook, whose attack was opened up by the disappearance of the pawn. This is an example of **discovered check,** a powerful and sometimes unexpected maneuver.

18 Qd1-a1   ...

Another attacking move by White. If Black makes a mistake,

White may take the Bishop on a2 next turn, since it is currently unprotected.

18   ...   Ba2-d5

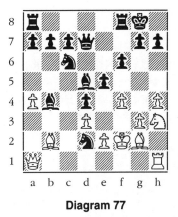

Diagram 77

STRATEGY WITH A WINNING ADVANTAGE

Black sees the attack and relocates the Bishop to d5, offering to exchange it for White's Bishop on g2. If White captures the Bishop, Black will recapture with the Queen on d7.

Why does Black want to exchange the Bishops? The answer is very important and is a key part of what is called *technique*. **Technique** is the method of converting an advantage into actual victory.

One rule of technique is this one: ***When ahead in material, try to exchange pieces***.

The reason for this is simple. Suppose you have seven pieces to your opponent's five. In that case, the five pieces may well be able to coordinate their efforts and put up a stout resistance. But if you are able to exchange off pieces until you have three and your opponent has only one, is much less likely that the one piece can beat off the three pieces.

Exchanging pieces when ahead is a powerful plan since it's so hard to for the other side to avoid.

In this position, for instance, there's no way White can avoid the exchange of Bishops. The only move to avoid trading Bishops is Bg2-f1, which would lose the Rook on h1 to the Black Bishop.

19   Rh1-c1   ...

White tries to activate his Rook by moving it out of the corner and onto the open c-file, where it would have some scope. This would normally be a good plan. Here, however, Black has guarded against this possibility with a nasty trap.

BLACK MARCHES ON

19   ...   Nd2-b3

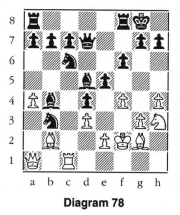

Diagram 78

Black responds with a **Knight fork**. The Knight attacks both the Queen on a1 and the Rook on c1. In this case, White will need to save his Queen, so he will likely lose his Rook for Black's Knight. Unless, that is, he finds a hidden resource in the position.

20   Bg2xd5 check ...

White's Bishop captures the Black Bishop, giving check to the Black King. Because Black must get out of check before doing anything else, he doesn't have time to capture the White Queen.

| 20 | ... | Qd7xd5 |

Black gets out of check by capturing the attacking Bishop.

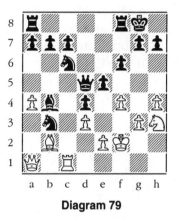

Diagram 79

| 21 | Qa1-b1 | ... |

White misses his chance! Do you see what he could have done instead? Look again at the last diagram.

White could have played Qa1-a2, a nice move which **pins** the Knight to the Black Queen. The Knight wouldn't be able to move, because if it did, White would be able to capture the Queen behind it.

For instance, if Black went ahead and played Nb3xc1, White would play Qa2xd5 check, capturing the Black Queen and giving check at the same time! After Black moved his King out of check, White could then play Bb2xc1, and he would have won a Knight and a Queen while losing only a Rook in return. That's a big gain for White, and it would have put him in control of the game.

Of course, Black probably wouldn't have permitted all this to happen. The simplest solution for him would be to guard the Queen by Ra8-d8. With the Queen guarded, Black would then be able to move the Knight next turn in safety. But then White would have time to move his threatened Rook.

At this point, you may well ask "Are chessplayers really able to see ahead like that?" The answer is yes. After you've been playing awhile, you'll be able to do it too. For now, you may want to actually move the pieces around on the board to see these possibilities as they develop. In awhile, you'll be able to visualize these variations in your head.

21	...	Nb3xc1

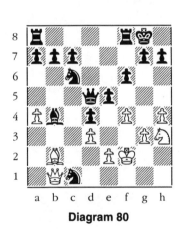

Diagram 80

Black pockets the Rook - the final booty from his early attack on the White Queenside.

22	f4xe5	...

THE FINAL ATTACKS
White should capture the Black Knight with Qb1xc1. He must feel he'll be able to get the Knight later, but events move too quickly now.

22 ... f6xe5 check

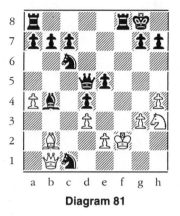

Diagram 81

Black announces check! Not from the lowly pawn that did the capturing, but from the powerful Rook back on f8. By stepping aside, the pawn opened up the Rook's line for a discovered check. White must now save his King.

23 Kf2-g1 ...

White had almost no choice. The e1 square is guarded by the Black Bishop on b4, while the e3 square is controlled by the Black pawn on d4. The f3 and f1 squares are also under attack by the Black Rook. Finally the g2 square is controlled by the Black Queen. That leaves only the g1 square that's safe for the King.

Now Black finds a nice combination to finish White off and put him out of his misery.

23 ... Rf8-f1 check

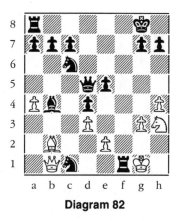

Diagram 82

The Black Rook swoops down and checks the White King. But hasn't Black overlooked something? The Rook is undefended!

    24   Kg1xf1   ...

White gets out of check by capturing the checking Rook. What's Black up to?

    24   ...   Qd5-h1 check

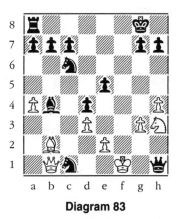

Diagram 83

This was it. Since the White King no longer guards the h1

square, the Queen moves in and takes up residence. Meanwhile the King is under attack again.

    25   Kf1-f2   ...

The King steps aside and evades the Queen's attack.

    25   ...   Bb4-e1 checkmate

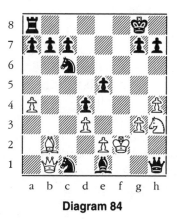

Diagram 84

The Bishop moves down to the first rank, attacking the King from the rear, and Black announces "Checkmate".

Is Black correct? Before you give up a game, check and make sure that your opponent's announcement of checkmate is right. He might be bluffing!

The Bishop attacks the King, and the King can't capture the Bishop since it's guarded by the Queen. The Black Queen also guards the squares f1, g1, g2, and f3. The squares e2 and g3 are blocked by White pawns, and finally the Black pawn at d4 guards the last escape square at e3. White has no piece that can capture the Black Bishop, and interposition is impossible. So White is checkmated, and the game is over.

ANALYZING THE GAME
Why did White lose the game?

The seeds of his defeat were planted in the first few moves. While Black was developing his pieces to active squares, White ceded control of the center with moves like d2-d3, f2-f3, h2-h4, and a2-a4. White was concerned with moving his pawns to protected squares, and not with using his pawns to control the center of the board.

By the time White was able to move a few pieces off the back row, Black was already in position to launch an attack. The attack, which started with Nf6-d5 and Bc5-b4, quickly netted some booty: White lost a Knight and a Rook while trying to save his King and Queen. After a few consolidating moves, Black was able to use the open files and diagonals around the White King to launch what we call a **mating attack**, an attack whose purpose is checkmate rather than just the gain of material.

The important lesson to be learned from this game is this: You must fight for the center of the board! Although moves around the edges of the board may look safe, you must reject them in favor of establishing equilibrium or even superiority in the center.

9. SAMPLE GAME - STRATEGY, TACTICS & MATE!

PREVIEW

Our first game was rather a one-sided affair, with Black establishing a quick superiority over his less experienced opponent and then cruising home to victory. This next game is a much more evenly matched struggle, with both players aware of the importance of the center and alert to the tactical possibilities in the position.

OPENING WITH THE QUEEN'S PAWN

	White	Black
1	d2-d4	...

An excellent way to start the game. White plants a pawn firmly in the center, opens up lines for his Bishop on c1 and his Queen, and renders the squares e5 and c5 off limits to Black's pieces. The only other move that accomplishes as much is e2-e4.

In general, opening with the Queen pawn is favored by players who want a slower game, with a gradual buildup to hostilities. Opening with the King pawn tends to be favored by buccaneers who like slashing action right from the beginning. But these are only generalizations, and it's easy for a Queen's pawn game to become a wild tactical affair, while King's pawn games can become sedate positional struggles.

If left to his own devices, White will continue next turn with e2-e4, grabbing all of the center for his own and putting Black in a cramped position. Black must prevent this.

1   ...   d7-d5

An excellent response on Black's part. By advancing his Queen's pawn, he ensures himself an equal share of the center. At the same time, he prevents White from continuing with e2-e4, which would give White a tremendous central position.

Another popular move at this point is Ng8-f6, developing the Knight and also preventing White from continuing with e2-e4. That moves leads to the so-called "Indian" defenses, like the **Nimzo-Indian**, **King's Indian**, and **Queen's Indian**, which became popular in master play in the 1920s and 1930s and have remained popular to this day. But d7-d5 is the classical way of responding to the Queen's pawn opening, and there's nothing wrong with it.

2   c2-c4   ...

Diagram 85

THE QUEEN'S GAMBIT

This move characterizes the **Queen's Gambit**. A gambit is an opening variation where one of the players (usually White) offers a pawn for the sake of some compensating advantage. In this case, White is offering up his c-pawn. Black is free to capture by d5xc4. In return, however, Black's pawn will give up control of the e4 square. White could then continue, either next turn or at some later point, with e2-e4 and grab a disproportionate share of the center.

The Queen's Gambit became a popular opening in the nineteenth century and has remained one of the mainstays of master chess ever since. Black has several ways to answer the gambit, all of which have advantages and disadvantages. With proper play on both sides, White should retain an initiative for a long time.

2	...	d5xc4

Diagram 86

Black responds in the most direct fashion - capturing the gambit pawn. He is willing to give up some control over the e4 square, but in return he has a solid pawn in his pocket.

Black has other possibilities. All of the following moves have been played in master practice, and all have advantages and disadvantages:

• e7-e6, leading to what's called the **Orthodox Defense**,

a very solid line.

- c7-c6, the **Slav Defense**, also solid but with more counter-attacking possibilities than the Orthodox.

- e7-e5, the **Albin Counter Gambit**, in which Black gambits a pawn for active play. In the 1930s and 1940s, this was a favorite of the American neo-Romantic school, led by Weaver Adams.

- Ng8-f6, aiming for active piece play but conceding White the pawn center.

The first two moves remain quite popular, while the last two are thought to be unsound.

EARLY STRATEGIC THINKING

Now that Black has chosen to take the pawn, what is proper strategy for both sides? White's strategy is easy to define:

- Develop his pieces.

- Try to recapture the pawn at a favorable opportunity.

- Aim to exploit the absence of the Black pawn at d5 by playing e2-e4 at a time when he can maintain a strong pawn center, with pawns on d4 and e4.

What about Black? Experience has shown that Black shouldn't make too much of an effort to hold onto his extra pawn. (If he does, White can gain an edge in development and a strong attack.) Black should try to develop his pieces with an eye on preventing White from setting up the strong pawn center at e4 and d4.

THE OPENING DEVELOPS

    3   Ng1-f3   ...

White is not in a hurry to recapture the pawn. (If he wanted to, he could have recaptured right away by playing 3 Qd1-a4 check and 4 Qa4xc4.) Instead he develops his Knight to its best square, defends his d4 pawn a second time, and puts additional pressure on the e5 square.

Another way of handling the opening is to play e2-e4 right away. This has become popular in master chess very recently, and leads to a sharp and exciting game.

3   ...   Ng8-f6

Black follows suit with a sound developing move of his own. The Knight moves off the back rank and aims at the e4 square, preventing White from playing e2-e4 immediately.

4   e2-e3   ...

Diagram 87

White can't push the pawn to e4 without losing it to the Black Knight, so White moves it one square instead. On e3, the pawn supports its brother on d4. In addition, the pawn move opens up a diagonal for the White Bishop, which now threatens to move out and capture the Black pawn on c4.

4   ...   e7-e6

99

A prudent decision. Black decides not to waste time protecting the c4 pawn, but instead elects to continue development. By moving his e-pawn, Black opens up a line of development for the Bishop on f8. Once that piece moves, Black will be in position to castle King-side, protecting the King and freeing the Rook.

Here's an example of the sort of problems Black can incur by trying too hard to hold onto the c4-pawn: Qd8-d5 (guarding the pawn with the Queen), 5 Nb1-c3 (attacking the Queen with the Knight) Qd5-c6 (trying to stay in touch with the pawn) 6 Nf3-e5 (double attack -- attacking the Queen and the pawn with the Knight) Qc6-d6 (moving the Queen away from the Knight's attack) 7 Bf1xc4 (winning back the pawn and attacking the pawn at f7 with the Bishop and the Knight). White has won back the pawn anyway, and in addition has three pieces dominating the center of the board, while Black is scrambling to find a safe place for the Queen.

5 Bf1xc4 ...

The Bishop enters the game by capturing the gambit pawn. In addition, the Bishop move clears the way for White to castle.

5 ...   c7-c5

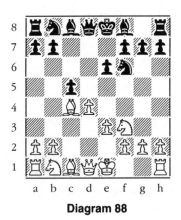

Diagram 88

Black strikes out at White's center by attacking his d-pawn.

Notice two features of Black's fifth move. First, unlike White's advance of the c-pawn, this is not a gambit. The Black c-pawn is protected by the Bishop on f8, so if White elects to capture the pawn, Black can immediately recapture with the Bishop.

Second, what Black is really attempting to do with this move is exchange a **wing pawn** (the c-pawn) for a **center pawn** (the d-pawn). In chess parlance, center pawns are the pawns on the d-file and e-file. Wing pawns are all the others. Since the center is so important, such an exchange is usually advantageous for the player giving up the wing pawn. It's also hard to avoid for the player with the center pawn. Once Black has played c7-c5, he can force the exchange at a later time.

Compare what's happening here to our first sample game. There, Black was given a completely free hand in the center and was soon able to build up a strong attack. In this game, both players are energetically contesting the center squares. As a result, neither player has achieved a decisive advantage there, and the game is evenly balanced.

6   0-0   ...

Castling - very good. White ignores the attack on his center, since his d-pawn is very securely protected, by the pawn at e3, the Knight at f3, and the Queen at d1. Instead, he uses his first opportunity to castle, which removes his King from the danger of the center to the relative peace and tranquility of the corner. At the same time, the Rook moves closer to the central files, where future action will occur.

6   ...   Bf8-e7

A quiet developing move, but effective nonetheless. The Bishop moves off the first rank, guards the Knight, and opens the back rank for castling.

In the opening, good moves don't have to be spectacular. Simple developing moves which prepare to coordinate the pieces for later action are usually the best way to start the game.

7   Qd1-c2   ...

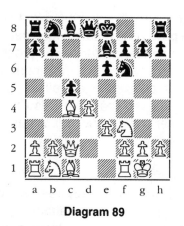

Diagram 89

A quiet move with a number of subtle points. The Queen moves off the first rank to a position of relative safety. By moving, the Queen vacates the square d1 for the White Rook at f1.

In addition, the Queen attacks the e4 square, supporting the pawn in case White wants to play e3-e4 at a later point.

CHECK! OR NOT TO CHECK!

The observant student will have noticed that White, instead of developing modestly to c2, could have given check with the Queen by playing Qd1-a4 check. "What's wrong with that?" you may ask. "Isn't it good to check when you can?"

The answer is - it depends. Is your opponent inconvenienced by your check? Does he have to move his King, and thereby lose the right to castle? If the answer to these questions is "yes", then a quick check in the opening is probably right. If, however, your opponent can block your check while developing pieces at the same time, checking may be a waste.

Suppose that White played Qd1-a4 check instead of Qd1-c2. The game might have continued like this: Black: Bc8-d7 (blocking the check and attacking the White Queen with the Bishop), 8 Qa4-c2 (running from the Bishop's attack) b7-b5 (the Black pawn attacks the White Bishop), 9 Bc4-d3 (dodges the attack) c5-c4 (attacks the Bishop again), 10 Bd3-e2 (avoids capture by the pawn) Bd7-c6.

Set up this sequence on your board and see what has happened. By attacking the White Queen and the White Bishop, forcing them to retreat, Black has gained tons of space and now controls the center and leads in development. Not a good result for the early Queen check! Better to keep the Queen close to home for now.

| 7 | ... | 0-0 |

Black safeties his King and brings the Rook closer to the center.

| 8 | d4xc5 | ... |

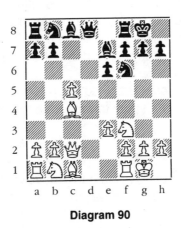

Diagram 90

THE PAWN TRAP
White captures the Black pawn on c5 and in the process sets a clever trap, prepared by his previous move of the Queen to c2. Do you see the trap?

The idea is this: Black's natural response is to recapture the pawn by Be7xc5. That, however, allows White to play the imaginative shot Bc4xe6! The White Bishop captures the pawn on e6 and, by moving, opens up the White Queen's attack on the undefended Black Bishop on c5. After Black plays Bc8xe6, White can respond with Qc2xc5. White will have given up his own Bishop but gained a pawn and a Bishop in return, netting a pawn.

What's all the fuss about a measly little pawn? Simply this - because of a pawn's ability to become a Queen, an advantage of just one pawn can be enough to win in the endgame. White's strategy would be very simple. He would look to exchange pieces at every opportunity, hoping to eventually reach an endgame with his King and six pawns opposed by Black's King and five pawns. In that situation, he would have good chances to push his extra pawn up the board and eventually make a Queen.

There's no guarantee that simple strategy would work, of course. Black wouldn't want to exchange pieces, and in the complicated fighting of the middle game, Black might succeed in outplaying White and win back his pawn, and even more. But the onus would be on Black to change the course of the game. White would have the upper hand and the easier time.

Meanwhile, what should Black do? If he sees the trap behind Be7xc5, what should he play to recapture the pawn?

8	...	Nb8-a6

Black sees the trap but plays instead a move which allows White to keep the captured pawn, if he plays correctly.

Black's idea is to attack the pawn a second time, while preventing White from supporting the pawn with b2-b4. (Black would simply capture on b4 with the Knight in that case.) While this looks clever, it doesn't really work, as we shall see.

Black had a couple of plays that would have eventually recaptured the pawn with a good game. One was Qd8-a5, attacking the pawn a second time, followed next turn by Qa5xc5. This would leave Black even in material with a solid position. Another way was a7-a5!, advancing the a-pawn to cut off support from the White b-pawn. Black could then pile up on the White pawn with developing moves like Nb8-a6, Qd8-c7, Bc8-d7, and Rf8-c8. Eventually Black would get the pawn back while developing his pieces in the process.

> 9   Bc4xa6!   ...

White captures the attacking Knight. At the same time, the Queen now defends the c5-pawn.

The exclamation mark after White's 9th move means that (in the annotator's opinion) his decision to capture the Black Knight was a good one.

> 9   ...   b7xa6

Black must recapture or be a Knight down.

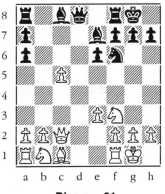

Diagram 91

10   c5-c6   ...

White advances the pawn another square, removing it from the Bishop's attack.

THE ISOLATED PAWN

Although the pawn may look menacing on the sixth rank, it's actually nothing for Black to be worried about. Since the pawn is so far away from the rest of White's army, it's a relatively simple matter for Black to surround and capture it.

White would have done better to support the pawn with another pawn by b2-b4. The pawn on b4 could then be strengthened next turn by a2-a3. White would then have a **pawn chain**, with pawns connected to each other on a3, b4, and c5. A chain like this is a very powerful formation, since Black's pieces would have difficulty attacking it. The best point to attack a chain is at its base, which is the one pawn in the chain not protected by other pawns. Here that base would be at a3, a point far removed from the Black pieces.

10   ...   Qd8-c7

The Queen stops the pawn dead in its tracks. Next Black will try to maneuver his pieces to pick it off.

11   b2-b3   ...

White is trying to get his pieces off the first rank in an orderly fashion. He can't play the most natural move, Nb1-c3, because the Knight on c3 would cut off the Queen's protection of the pawn at c6, so Black would just reply with Qc7xc6. The idea of b2-b3 is to develop the Bishop at b2. From that square it would guard e5, so White could then follow up with Nf3-e5, guarding the pawn at c6.

It's a clever plan, but too slow. Events can move quickly on the chess board. Probably White would have been better off just developing his Bishop on d2 and then swinging his Rook from f1 to c1 to guard the pawn again.

THE PIN!

11	...	Bc8-b7!

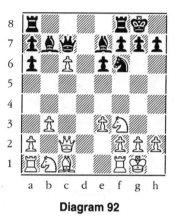

Diagram 92

Black counters with a surprising move which illustrates the strength of a **pin**. Notice that if White plays c6xb7, Black's Queen on c7 will swoop down and capture the undefended White Queen on c2. True, White could then play b7xa8 (Q), capturing the Black Rook and promoting to a new Queen, but Black would immediately capture the new White Queen with his Rook on f8.

The upshot of all these exchanges would be bad for White: he would have lost his Queen and the pawn on c6 (total value 10 points) for Black's Bishop and Rook in the corner (total value 8 points).

Rather than submit to that trade, White will have to leave the Bishop alone. But what to do? Black now attacks the advanced pawn with his Queen and Bishop, while White only defends it with his Queen. If White does nothing, Black will snap off the pawn next turn.

12   Nf3-d4   ...

The Knight moves to a secure spot in the center to defend the pawn a second time.

12   ...   Ra8-c8

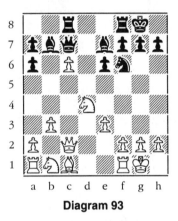

Diagram 93

Black piles up on the pawn a third time and continues to exploit the pin against the White Queen. Black now attacks the pawn a third time (with the Bishop, Queen, and Rook), while White can only defend it twice (with the Queen and Knight).

A quick rule-of-thumb in chess is this: if you attack a pawn or piece more times than it is defended, you can profitably capture it. That's the case here. Black threatens to play the following sequence: 13 ... Bb7xc6 (Bishop takes the pawn), 14 Nd4xc6 (Knight recaptures) Qc7xc6 (Queen recaptures), 15 Qc2xc6 (Queen captures) Rc8xc6 (Rook recaptures).

That's a lot of bloodletting, with the final result that Black has captured a pawn, Knight, and Queen while losing a Queen and Bishop in return. Net profit for Black: one pawn. White can't really avoid this, since he has no more pieces that can move to defend the pawn.

13   Bc1-a3   ...

Seeing that he can't defend the pawn a third time, White sets a little trap. His Bishop now attacks Black's Bishop, which is currently defended by Black's Queen. If Black starts the capturing sequence outlined in the last note, his Queen will no longer be on c7 when the sequence is done. White would end up the sequence by capturing on e7 with his Bishop, winding up a Bishop ahead. (See if you can work this out by yourself.)

It's a clever idea, but Black can easily foil it.

13   ...   Be7xa3

Good move! By first capturing the White Bishop, Black eliminates the problem. Then he'll be free to proceed with the capturing sequence.

14   Nb1xa3   ...

White has to recapture or he'll be a Bishop behind.

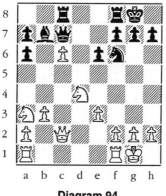

Diagram 94

14   ...   Bb7xc6

Black initiates the sequence to capture the White pawn.

    15   Nd4xc6   ...

Seeing nothing better, White agrees to the exchanges.

    15   ...   Qc7xc6

Black must recapture of course.

    16   Qc2xc6   ...

White doesn't have to exchange Queens, but he doesn't like the look of the middle game that would result if he retreated his Queen to somewhere like b2 or e2. In that case, Black would play Rf8-d8 and have a solid lead in development, with all four of his pieces mobilized and bearing on the center, while White's two Rooks were still in the corners. That wouldn't necessarily be fatal, but White decides to avoid the possibility and head for the ending.

    16   ...   Rc8xc6

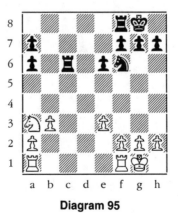

Diagram 95

MID-GAME ANALYSIS

Take a look at that last diagram, and you'll see that the situation on the board has changed dramatically. Most of the pieces are gone: only two Rooks and a Knight remain on each side. What's going on? How should the players plan future operations?

The first thing to notice is that we've moved very quickly through the first two phases of our chess game. Our opening probably ended around move 10, when White played c5-c6. In the next few moves, Black piled up on the pawn and won it, restoring material equality. Our middle game was very brief, extending from moves 10-16. Most of the pieces were exchanged off on the c6 square. Now we're in the endgame.

Who has the advantage? White. Why? Curiously, because of those two innocent-looking Black pawns on a6 and a7. They're called *doubled, isolated* pawns, and they're weak in the endgame.

Doubled pawns are two pawns of the same color together on the same file, as a result of an earlier capture. **Isolated pawns** are pawns that can't be defended by pawns on adjacent files. The a-pawns are doubled because there are two of them on the a-file. They're isolated because there is no pawn on the b-file to defend them. That means they can only be defended by other pieces, and that could be troublesome. You don't want your powerful pieces tied down to defending weak pawns, because you'll then be thrown back on the defensive.

White's plan is to attack the Black a-pawns and try to win one or both of them. Black will have to prevent this somehow. To win, however, White will have to mobilize his Rooks.

In the endgame, the Rooks really come into their own. Since pawns have been stripped away and ranks and files now lie open, the Rooks can swing into action, penetrate into the enemy position, and cause real havoc.

> 17   Rf1-d1   ...

A good start. The White Rook seizes control of the open d-file. Notice that this move prevents Black from moving either Rook to the d-file, since White would then capture it.

	17	...	Nf6-e4

The Knight is actively placed on this square, but at a cost. Notice that the Black Knight, when located on f6, prevented the White Rook from penetrating to d7. By moving to e4, Black gives up control of this vital square.

	18	Rd1-d7!	...

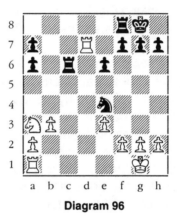

Diagram 96

White immediately takes advantage of Black's last move by penetrating into the heart of Black's position.

In the endgame, Rooks belong on the seventh rank. White's seventh rank is the squares a7 to h7. Black's seventh rank is the squares a2 to h2. A Rook on the seventh rank performs two functions. Its long-range attacking power enables it to threaten all the pawns along the rank. Right now the Rook is attacking the pawns at a7 and f7. If the pawn at f7 moves, the Rook's influence will reach over to the pawn at g7, and so on. Its second function is to constrain the enemy King.

Since the King usually sits on the first row (a8 to h8, in the case of the Black King), a Rook on the seventh can keep the enemy King pinned to that row, especially if the pawns have been advanced.

White's immediate threat is to capture the Black pawn at a7, which would place him one pawn ahead. Black needs to counter that threat.

COUNTER-ATTACK

18   ...   Rf8-c8!

Black counters threat with threat. Do you see why White can't capture the pawn on a7?

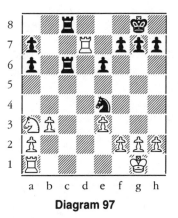

Diagram 97

If White goes ahead and plays Rd7xa7, here's what would happen. Black would move his Rook down to White's first rank with check: Rc6-c1 check! White would capture: Ra1xc1. Black would then recapture: Rc8xc1 checkmate! The Rook would attack White's King, and the King's two escape squares (f1 and h1) would also be under attack by Black's Rook.

No escape, no interposition, and no capture spells checkmate. This is an example of the **back-rank mate,** which we discussed in our chapter on tactics.

White, however, sees the threat. Now he needs a good defense.

> 19 Na3-c4!   ...

Excellent. White defends against the threat with a developing move. The Knight takes up a secure outpost in the center and cuts off the Black Rooks from their attack on White's first rank.

This move illustrates another weakness associated with doubled pawns. If the Black pawn at a6 were on its original file, say at b6, then Black could chase the Knight away by moving his pawn to b5 and attacking the Knight. But as is, no Black pawn can harass the Knight, and the Rook doesn't want to capture since the Knight is guarded by the White pawn at b3. (If Black captured, he would lose a Rook (5 points) for a Knight (3 points) - a bad trade.)

> 19 ...   Rc6-c7

Cut off from the attack, the Rook moves back to block the White Rook's attack on the pawn at a7. The Black Rooks securely protect each other.

> 20 Ra1-d1   ...

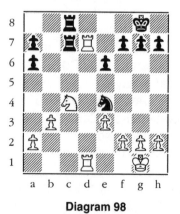

Diagram 98

ACTIVE VS. PASSIVE CHESS

In chess, it's almost always better to play *actively* rather than *passively*. Active play means finding moves which counter your opponent's threats with new threats of your own. Remember that when you make a threat, there's no guarantee that your opponent will see it. When your opponent doesn't see your threat, you may get to win the game right here on the spot.

Black's threat was to capture the White Rook on d7. Of course, it's easy for White to defend against this threat. He could capture Black's Rook with his own, after which Black would recapture; or he could retreat his Rook to safety. But his actual move was much better. Besides protecting his Rook, he sets up a new threat: Rd7-d8 check. Black would have to respond with Rc8xd8, then White would reply Rd1xd8 checkmate! - another example of a back-row mate.

This is not a hard threat to see, and we can expect that Black will guard against it. But remember, your opponents aren't perfect, and sometimes they will err. Make sure you at least give them the opportunity.

| 20 | ... | h7-h5 |

As expected, Black guards against the back-row mate in a standard way. He moves one of the pawns in front of his King, providing the King with an escape square (in this case, h7). In chess, providing an escape square is known as **creating luft**.

| 21 | Rd7xc7 | ... |

White exchanges Rooks, reducing the number of pieces. White hopes that with just one pair of Rooks on the board, he will have an easier time trying to win one of the Black a-pawns.

| 21 | ... | Rc8xc7 |

Black must recapture.

22   Rd1-d3   ...

It's not clear what White intends by this move. In any case, it is not an easy matter for him to make progress, since Black's pieces guard the squares d7 and d6.

22   ...   a6-a5

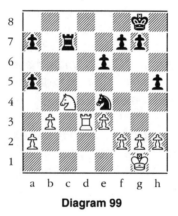

Diagram 99

Apparently a clever move. Black sees that White cannot immediately capture the pawn with his Knight. (If White plays Nc4xa5??, Black responds with Rc7-c1 check, after which White can only interpose his Rook, and then Black captures the Rook, giving checkmate - yet another back-row mate.)

Black's idea is to push the pawn again next turn, with a5-a4. This move will attack the White pawn on b3. That pawn will have to stay where it is to guard the White Knight, so it can't capture on a4. Black will then play a4xb3, and after White recaptures (a2xb3), Black will have exchanged one of his weak a-pawns for the White pawn on a2. This will eliminate the strategical weakness in his game, and produce a dead-even position.

That's the idea, and it's indeed a clever one. But it has a weakness, and White is about to spot the weakness and exploit

116

it with a clever combination.

COMBINATIONS

As you play chess, you'll hear a lot about combinations. Basically, a **combination** is a forced series of moves, leading to checkmate or a gain of material.

When you start playing chess, presumably against other beginners, you won't really need to play combinations to win. It will be enough to simply attack your opponent's pieces. Your opponent won't see all these attacks, and sometimes you'll just capture pieces that he forgot to defend. However, as you and your opponents gain experience, this simple-minded approach won't work anymore. He'll see your basic threats, just as you'll see his. You'll need to escalate your ability to generate threats, and that's where combinations come in.

In this game, White is about to play a combination to win the a5 pawn without getting checkmated in return. Let's see how he does it.

> 23   f2-f3!   ...

The first link in the combinational chain. White's move accomplishes two things: it provides luft for the White King at f2, and it attacks the Black Knight, forcing it to move.

> 23   ...   Ne4-c5

The Knight moves to a square where it attacks the White Rook. This saves the pawn for now, since White has to save his Rook.

> 24   Rd3-d8 check!...

The Rook saves itself by giving check at the same time. Black can't worry about his a5 pawn now. He *must* save the King.

> 24   ...   Kg8-h7

117

The King escapes, using the luft square created a few moves ago.

25   Nc4xa5   ...

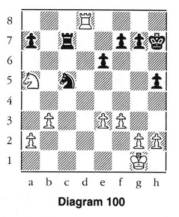

Diagram 100

THE PAWN IS CAPTURED

Success! White has captured the pawn, and Black has no counter-threats. With good play, White should eventually be able to win the game with his extra pawn. But that's still a long way off.

25   ...   Nc5-b7

Black moves his Knight and attacks both the White Knight and White Rook. If White doesn't notice that either of these pieces is attacked, he may lose one of them.

THE EXCHANGE

26   Na5xb7   ...

White sees the threat and captures the Black Knight with his own.

26   ...   Rc7xb7

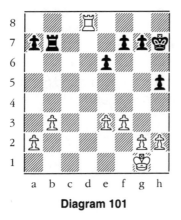

Diagram 101

Who has benefitted from this exchange? The answer is -White. In general, the side that's ahead in material wants to exchange pieces, in order to simplify to an endgame that's relatively uncomplicated and easy to win. The side that's behind in material, on the other hand, wants to keep as many pieces on the board as possible, to create threats and complications. With many pieces roaming around the board, the leader is more likely to overlook a potential danger somewhere.

ENDGAME OBJECTIVES
Now that we're far into the endgame, what should the players' objectives be? Let's start with White.

White's goals can be summarized as follows:

> (1) Develop and centralize the remaining pieces. That means the Rook should control one of the central files, while the King should be brought to the center as well- preferably a square like d4 or c4.

> (2) If at all possible, Exchange Rooks. This will make the win much simpler.

119

(3) Attack a weakness in Black's position and tie the Black pieces down to defending it. One potential weakness is the pawn at a7. Other potential weaknesses may appear on the King-side as time goes by.

(4) Advance the pawns and penetrate with the King into the heart of Black's position.

(5) Win more pawns.

(6) Advance a pawn and Queen it.

(7) Checkmate the Black King.

While doing all this, White has to watch out for Black counterthreats and guard against them. Remember - your opponent gets to make threats too.

How about Black? He will also try to centralize his pieces, must mostly his goal is to make White's job as difficult as possible. This means he has to stay alert, and look for the chance to set traps.

THE END GAME IN MOTION

Let's see how the players carry out their objectives.

27   Kg1-f2!   ...

Very good. White's Rook is already well posted, so White begins the job of bringing his King to the center.

27   ...   Rb7-c7!

Also very good. Black's relocation of the Rook is a multi-purpose move. The Rook seizes control of one of the two open files, and threatens to move to c2 next turn with check. The check would force White to move his King, after which Black could take the pawn on a2.

28   Rd8-d2   ...

White guards the second rank with his Rook, thus preventing Black's Rook from penetrating.   The Rook still controls the central d-file from its more modest post.

28   ...   f7-f5

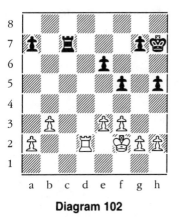

Diagram 102

This looks aggressive but doesn't really threaten anything. Black should be aware of a simple fact: the farther back his pawns are, the more difficult it is for White to attack them. The more advanced his pawns, the easier they are to attack.

The logic here is simple. Consider the two Black pawns which used to be on e6 and f7. Since the f7 pawn guarded the e6 pawn, White, in order to make a credible threat, had to attack the pawn on f7. Now that the pawns are on e6 and f5, White can attack the e6 pawn instead.

A better move was to start to centralize the King with Kh7-g6.

29   f3-f4   ...

This move takes control of e5 and g5. White would like to *fix* Black's pawns in position. This will make them more vulnerable to attack later.

29   ...   Kh7-g6

A good move, getting the King closer to the central files.

30   Kf2-f3   ...

White is planning to get the King to the center by playing e3-e4, and then, if Black captures on e4, to recapture with his King.

30   ...   Kg6-f6

Black continues to centralize.

31   h2-h4   ...

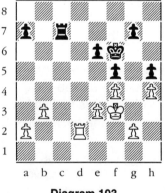

Diagram 103

White is trying to prevent Black from playing his pawn from g7-g5. By playing f3-f4 and h2-h4, he has ruled out this possibility entirely.

GOOD MOVES AND BAD MOVES
This isn't really a bad idea, and White should still be winning the game. But his pawn moves indicate that he's getting distracted from his main idea, which should be centralizing his King and

threatening Black's weak pawn on a6. This is actually fairly typical of endgame play between inexperienced players: they often get wrapped up in skirmishes around the board, and lose sight of the big picture for awhile.

31	...	Rc7-b7

An odd move. The Rook was well-placed on c7: it controlled the open c-file and guarded Black's second rank, including the weak pawns on a7 and g7. In fact, c7 was the *ideal* defensive square for the Rook right now. In addition, on c7 the Rook was poised to jump into White's position at c2, should White ever move his Rook off his second row.

On b7, the Rook is not nearly so well placed. It attacks a White pawn (b3) which is securely protected by another pawn, and it no longer threatens to penetrate into White's camp.

A better move was just Kf6-e7. The King would be closer to the center and would guard the squares d8, d7, and d6, thus keeping out White's Rook. Here's a generally good motto: if you've determined that one of your pieces is on its ideal square, **leave it there**. Don't move it around just to have something to do.

32	Rd2-d6!	...

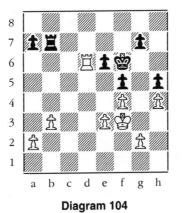

Diagram 104

A good, active move. White penetrates into Black's position, attacks the weak pawn at e6, and threatens to swing over to a6, where it would attack both weak pawns, at a7 and e6.

BLUNDER!!

32	...	Rb7-b6??

A terrible error which costs Black the game. As we said before, when you're behind in material, you want to keep as many pieces on the board as possible, to create difficulties and complications for your opponent. When you're ahead in material, you should be striving to exchange pieces off. Black is playing into White's hands with this move, as White would like nothing better than to exchange Rooks and play an endgame with just Kings and pawns.

Still, it's an easy blunder to understand. White's Rook is an active and bothersome piece, and Black has probably grown tired of defending against its threats. This move looks like an easy way out: "The Rook is annoying me. I'll trade it off." In chess, however, it pays to keep in mind the big picture.

33	Rd6xb6	...

White understands the general principle involved in these endings, and trades off the Rooks in a shot.

33	...	a7xb6

No choice, of course.

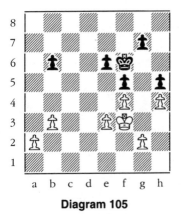

Diagram 105

WHITE'S END GAME STRATEGY

We've now reached an endgame where all the pieces have been traded off except the two Kings. White has six pawns, Black only five. White should be able to win pretty easily from this position. But what is his proper strategy?

White's basic strategy is as follows. Take a look at the left-hand side of the board. There White has what is called a **pawn majority**: two White pawns opposed by only one Black pawn. White will advance his two pawns together, eventually trading one of his pawns for Black's lone pawn on b6.

This trade will create a **passed pawn**: a pawn unopposed by any enemy pawn on its march to the Queening square. Since no other Black piece can stop it, the Black King will have to move to that side of the board to capture the White pawn.

This, however, will leave the pawns on the right-hand side of the board undefended. The White King will move in amongst these pawns, capturing a few and creating new passed pawns, which will then march on to Queen. With a new Queen, White will effect a quick checkmate.

Does that sound complicated? It's really not. Let's see how White carries out the plan.

THE MARCHING PAWNS

    34   a2-a4!   ...

Very good. White starts his pawns marching.

    34   ...   Kf6-e7

Black can't allow White to get a new Queen. His King moves over to block the pawns.

    35   b3-b4   ...

The pawn moves to b4 so White can play a4-a5 next turn.

    35   ...   Ke7-d6

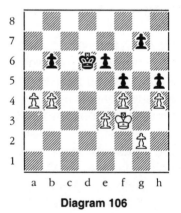

Diagram 106

The King moves closer to the pawns.

    36   e3-e4!   ...

A move with several purposes. To begin with, the pawn seizes control of d5, preventing Black from moving his King to that powerful central square. If Black exchanges, the White King will recapture and move closer to the center. Also, White may want to exchange with e4xf5 at some point in the future, if Black does not.

36 ... Kd6-c6

Black doesn't want to exchange and let White's King go to a better square (e4). Instead he shuffles his King and awaits developments.

37 Kf3-e3 ...

If Black won't exchange, White still wants to move his King to a better square. He's headed for d4, where he can either threaten to attack the King-side (via e5) or support the advance of his Queen-side pawns via a4-a5.

37 ... Kc6-b7

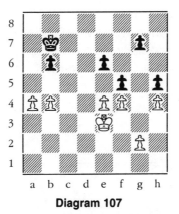

Diagram 107

It's not clear what the King is doing on this square. Black would have done better to just play back to the central square d6.

38 e4xf5 ...

White clears away a couple of pawns to prepare his King's advance.

38 ...   e6xf5

Black must recapture.

39 Ke3-d4 ...

The King starts to penetrate Black's position. He's headed for e5 and the defenseless Black pawns.

39 ...   Kb7-a6

Black is trying to attack the White pawns, but he can't make much progress.

40 Kd4-e5 ...

Threatens to take the Black pawn on f5 next turn.

40 ...   b6-b5

Black makes a threat of his own. He's hoping White will be distracted and continue with Ke5xf5, after which Black would play b5xa4, and eventually his pawn on a4 would march down to a1 and Queen. However, White is alert and parries this threat

41 a4-a5! ...

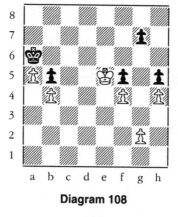

Diagram 108

WHITE GETS A DECISIVE EDGE

White avoids Black's little trap by the simple expedient of pushing his pawn. (a4xb5, exchanging pawns, would also have won, but a little more slowly.) By playing to a5, White has created what is called a **protected passed pawn**, a pawn which is both passed (because no enemy pawn opposes it) and protected (in this case, supported by its own pawn on b4). Such a pawn is very dangerous because it can only be stopped from Queening by the Black King himself.

In order to catch the White pawn before it can Queen, the Black King must stay in an area called the **square** of the pawn. In this position, the square of the White a-pawn is the block of squares from a5 to a8 to d8 to d5. (See next diagram.)

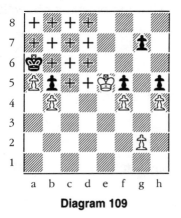

Diagram 109

As long as the Black King is on one of the squares marked by a '+', it's in position to stop the White pawn if it tries to Queen. If the King is outside that square, White would be able to play a5-a6 and Queen the pawn. (Try putting the Black King on different squares and verify this for yourself.)

With the Black King confined to that narrow space, however, how can it guard the other Black pawns on the f, g, and h-files from White's marauding King? It can't, and that spells doom.

In the actual game, Black conceded at this point, recognizing that White's advantage was now large enough to ensure victory. However, we're going to play the game out to a conclusion, to gain some experience in how chess games are actually won. After all, not all your opponents will be gracious enough to give up, so you'll need to know how to deliver the *coup de grace*.

THE COUP DE GRACE!

41   ...   g7-g6

Black defends the pawn on f5.

42   Ke5-f6   ...

White moves to capture the pawn on g6, which now can't be defended.

42   ...   Ka6-b7

The Black King moves closer.

43   Kf6xg6   ...

White nets another pawn and destroys the defender of f5 and h5.

43   ...   Kb7-c7

Black moves closer.

44   Kg6xf5   ...

White is now three pawns ahead and has another passed pawn (f5).

44   ...   Kc7-d7

Black is trying to stop both White pawns.

45   Kf5-g6   ...

The White King moves aside to let the f-pawn advance.

45   ...   Kd7-e7

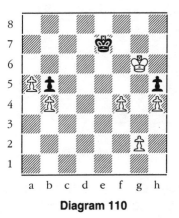

Diagram 110

Black moves closer to the f-pawn, to try to get in front of it with his King. But meanwhile...

46   a5-a6!   ...

Black has moved his King outside the square of the a-pawn, which begins its dash for a8.

46   ...   Ke7-d7

Black heads back the other way.

47   a6-a7   ...

Getting closer.

47   ...   Kd7-c7

Can't get there in time.

48   a7-a8 (Q)   ...

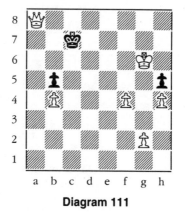

Diagram 111

White's pawn becomes a Queen, and he now has enough ammunition to play directly for checkmate.

48   ...   Kc7-d6

Black's King tries to stay in the center of the board. It's harder to checkmate him there than in the corner or on the edge.

49   Kg6-f6

White can't checkmate with the Queen alone; he will need his King as well. This move brings the King closer to the enemy King.

49   ...   Kd6-d7

Black's King stays as centralized as possible.

50   Qa8-a6   ...

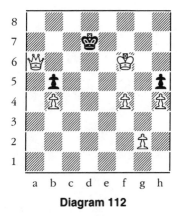

Diagram 112

The Queen takes control of the sixth rank, confining the Black King to rows 7 and 8. This is an essential part of the process of eventually confining him to the edge of the board, where checkmate will be delivered.

     50   ...   Kd7-c7

Staying off the edge.

     51   Kf6-e6   ...

Confining the Black King further. Notice that White is not checking the Black King, but simply restricting his movement to a more and more confined space.

     51   ...   Kd7-d8

Black has been forced to the eighth rank.

     52   Qa6-b7   ...

Leaves the King only one square.

     52   ...   Kd8-e8

Forced. No other legal move.

53   Qb7-e7 checkmate

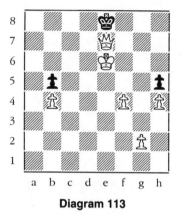

Diagram 113

The end. The White Queen attacks the Black King and in addition attacks all the squares around the Black King. The Queen is herself guarded by the White King, so she is immune from capture. Black has no way to get out of check, so the game is over.

10. JOINING A CHESS CLUB

The best way to get involved in chess is to join a chess club. There are chess clubs in all major cities (usually several) and at least one in most suburban areas. At a chess club, you'll meet people who share your interest in the game, you'll get to match wits against a wide variety of opponents, and you'll learn about local and regional tournaments.

In large cities, the major clubs are often open seven days a week. Smaller clubs in outlying areas might meet weekly in a school, church basement, or YMCA. Many clubs run weekly blitz tournaments, which is chess played at high speed - a few seconds per move or five minutes for the whole game. They're very exciting and a lot of fun for everyone. Clubs also run slower tournaments, perhaps on a monthly basis, and most clubs also have a club championship once a year.

To find out the location of clubs in your area, consult your local newspaper. If it runs a weekly chess column, that will usually contain news of local clubs. If your paper has a weekly "Calendar" or "Events" section, look in there. That's usually a low-cost place for clubs to advertise.

STARTING A NEW CLUB
You may live in an area that doesn't already have a chess club. Don't be discouraged! A club is easy to start. All you need is a place to play on a regular basis (once or twice a week is good), and a group of people who share your enthusiasm for the game.

A good way to start is to contact the U.S. Chess Federation, which is the governing body for chess in the United States. The USCF, as it's called, will be happy to send you information on starting a club. Write to them at 186 Route 9W, New Windsor, NY 12553.

11. TOURNAMENTS, RATINGS, & THE CHESS CLOCK

There are many thousands of chess tournaments held all around the world each year. Most are tiny local events, involving just a few players from the same club or city, often lasting no more than a single evening. Others are gigantic extravaganzas with hundreds or thousands of players, extending over a week or two. And a few are elite gatherings of the world's strongest grandmasters, at exclusive resorts, with prize funds running into hundreds of thousands of dollars.

The most exclusive event of all is the **World Championship** match itself, held only every two or three years, where the current World Champion is required to defend his title against the strongest challenger, for a purse that has reached as high as five million dollars.

In the United States, the biggest tournaments are the **U.S. Open**, held every August in a different city; the **New York Open**, held in April in New York; and the **National Open**, held in Las Vegas between Christmas and New Year's. Each of these tournaments attracts several hundred players from around the country, and each lasts about a week.

CHESS RATINGS

Almost all tournaments in the United States are *rated*, and players are assigned a numerical rating after playing in their first tournament. *Ratings* are a measure of your current playing strength; they range in value from about 800, which would indicate a complete beginner, to about 2800, which is World

Champion Gary Kasparov's rating. As you play in tournaments, your rating rises and falls with your results. If you exceed your expectation, your rating will rise; after a poor result it will fall.

Here's a summary of the different rating classes in chess tournaments:

Above 2500:	Grandmaster
Above 2400:	U.S. Senior Master
Above 2200:	Master
Above 2000:	Expert
Above 1800:	Class A
Above 1600:	Class B
Above 1400:	Class C
Above 1200:	ClassD
Below 1200:	Class E

Most newcomers to chess tournament start in Class D or E, then work there way up the ladder.

THE CHESS CLOCK

In tournaments, chess games are played with a **chess clock**, a device with two clock faces connected to each other. All games have a time limit (for instance, 30 moves in one hour), and players must complete the requisite number of moves in the stipulated time or forfeit the game.

To start a game, the player with the Black pieces presses a button to start the clock of the player with the White pieces. His clock continues to run, recording his elapsed time, until he makes a move and presses his button, which stops his clock and starts his opponent's clock.

Play continues in this fashion throughout the game, with each player's clock recording only the amount of time they have consumed. If a player uses more time than allotted, his **flag** (an indicator on the clock) falls and he loses the game.

TOUCH MOVE RULE

All tournament games are played using the **touch-move** rule, which we mentioned earlier in the book. If you touch a piece, you must move that piece if legally possible.

CHESS TOURNAMENTS

To learn more about chess tournaments in your area, contact the U.S. Chess Federation at the address given in the section on clubs. They can send you a sample copy of their magazine, **Chess Life**, with contains complete tournament listings around the country.

KASPAROV CHESS TRAVELLER™
THE HAND-HELD PORTABLE CHESS COMPUTER!

POWERFUL AND FUN

34 level/setting combinations including 16 playing levels makes an unbeatable choice for beginning and casual players. Convenient, economic and powerful (8K program), the Kasparov Traveller™ actually makes some very real human errors.

Even beginners have a chance to win! Knows all common chess rules and has features like 6 full move take-backs. Suggests moves if you get stuck, rejects illegal moves.

GREAT TRAVEL COMPANION

Ideal as a travel chess computer, its easy to learn and use. Knows all common chess rules and has features like 6 full move take-backs. Turn off at any time and continue play later - computer remembers position.

To order, send $69.95 to: Cardoza Publishing, PO Box 1500, Cooper Station, NY, NY 10276

TOURNAMENT-SYLE CHESS EQUIPMENT
Our Recommended Chess Shop

TOURNAMENT-SYLE CHESS CLOCKS - *by Jerger , the finest chess clocks made*
The elite and dependable Jerger chess clocks are fine precision made instruments **used worldwide** for tournament play and home use. Two **precision** mechanical clocks are housed together in a durable case and work as follows: The clocks are pre-set for the time limit in the game, and after one player has moved, he hits the button on his side of the clock. This button stops his clock while simultaneously starting his opponents. Likewise, when the opponent has moved, he hits his button to stop his clock and start the other one. Great for tournament play, and especially five minute chess! We have two clocks for you to choose from:
1. Tournament Player - Hard plastic housing - $89.95
2. Tournament Pro - Handsome, wooden housing - $149.95

TOURNAMENT-SYLE CHESS PIECES - *European craftsmanship*
All our pieces are guaranteed against defects and will provide quality play for years to come
The Staunton look is the classic and standard design for chess pieces.
3. Standard Staunton - A solid basic set made of wood with king 3 1/2 inches high. Weighted and felted. $39.95.
4. Tournament Staunton - Hand-crafted from maple with natural and walnut finish, these handsome pieces give you the tournament feel. Heavily weighted and felted - the king is 3 1/2 inches high. Our most popular pieces. $79.95.

CHESS BOARDS - *European craftsmanship*
5. Standard Board - Solid design features inlaid sycomore and walnut. Good basic choice for a casual set.1 9/16" squares. $34.95.
6. Tournament Board - Beautiful high-polished wooden board inlaid with maple and walnut. Finished on four sides. Four felt points on back protects tables. Two inch squares. $79.95.

30 DAY MONEY BACK GUARANTEE
We're sure you'll love our quality sets and clocks from our chess shop, but if for any reason you're unhappy, we'll gladly refund your purchase price in full within 30 days of purchase.

TOURNAMENT-SYLE CHESS CLOCKS

Tournament Player   *Tournament Pro*

TOURNAMENT-SYLE CHESS PIECES

Tournament Staunton

(Standard Staunton - Not Shown)

TOURNAMENT-SYLE CHESS BOARDS

Tournament Board

(Standard Board - Not Shown)